The Natural

How to Effortlessly Attract the Women You Want

The Natural

Richard La Ruina

Vermilion
LONDON

1 3 5 7 9 10 8 6 4 2

Published in 2013 by Vermilion, an imprint of Ebury Publishing
A Random House Group company

First published in the USA by HarperOne,
an imprint of HarperCollins Publishers in 2012

The Random House Group Limited Reg. No. 954009
Addresses for companies within the Random House Group can be found at
www.randomhouse.co.uk

A CIP catalogue record for this book is available from the British Library

Images used in this book are from the author and are used by permission.

ISBN 9780091948139

Copies are available at special rates for bulk orders. Contact the sales
development team on 020 7840 8487 for more information.

To buy books by your favourite authors and register for offers, visit
www.randomhouse.co.uk

The Random House Group Limited supports The Forest Stewardship
Council® (FSC®), the leading international forest-certification organisation.
Our books carrying the FSC label are printed on FSC®-certified paper.
FSC is the only forest-certification scheme supported by the leading
environmental organisations, including Greenpeace. Our
paper procurement policy can be found at
www.randomhouse.co.uk/environment

Printed and bound in Great Britain by Clays Ltd, St Ives PLC

Contents

The Invitation

Hundreds of Europe's most beautiful women crowd the dimly lit nightclub – each dressed more provocatively than the next, each looking to let loose. Ava, a five-foot-ten Estonian fashion model I met just minutes before, lays her head on my shoulder.

'It feels like I've known you my whole life,' she confides.

I smile and give her a reassuring hug. We've now reached what I call the point of no return. She's mine and I know it. Just a few short years ago, I'd never have been in a situation like this. I would have been at home with my mum, playing *Street Fighter*, eating Coco Pops on a Friday night. But now, life is different. *Very* different.

Five nights a week I go out. Five nights a week I have the opportunity to go home with a beautiful woman. What's changed? The short answer: everything. The slightly lengthier answer: I became a pickup artist … a very, very good one. And now I'm going to make you one too.

I don't care what you look like, how much money you make or how old you are. If you can follow simple directions and are willing to put in a little bit of work, I can promise you a new life. A life filled with beautiful women, incredible relationships and of course … lots of sex.

How can I make such a promise? Simple. Just like riding a bike, driving a car or kicking a football, meeting women and making them fall for you quickly is a *skill*. At first, it might seem hard … even impossible. But once you learn the proper technique and put in some practice, you can do it over and over again – effortlessly, naturally and easily. To date, I've shared this skill set with hundreds of thousands of men around the world, and if I know one thing to be true it's this: anyone can become a natural at the art of seduction. All you've got to do is *want it*. I'll supply the rest.

In the pages that follow I'll lay out for you, step by step, the methods and techniques that will give you power, choice and control over your love life – attributes that until now you probably didn't realise were possible.

But before I do, there's something you need to understand. What you're about to read is not theory or guesswork; it's not stuff I came up with by sitting around and thinking about what women might or might not like. There's enough of that out there already, and it's crap.

Instead, what you're about to discover is all field-tested and battle-proven. It's what I've *personally* discovered through my years of going out – night after night, day after day – working endlessly to figure out what works … and what doesn't.

I've done the hard work *for* you. I've endured the thousands of rejections it took before I finally figured out what worked, and now all *you've* got to do is read this book and then do what I say.

The results will follow. I guarantee it.

How to Read This Book

In coaching thousands of students since 2007, I've learned how to structure my teachings for maximum impact. Reflecting that experience, this book is organised in a very specific manner, the goal of which is to give you, the reader, the quickest possible route to mastery over the natural art of seduction.

Because of this, I urge you, please, do *not* skip, skim or flip through the pages in hopes of finding a magic 'pickup line'. If you do, I guarantee you will not find what you are looking for.

Instead, read this book from cover to cover, taking in each section in the correct order, allowing each piece to build upon the previous.

You will begin with 'From Geek to Natural'. This is my personal story of transformation from a twenty-three-year-old who had kissed only one girl, to someone whom many now consider one of the world's top seducers.

My road to mastery was not easy. I started in a very dark place and had all the chips stacked against me. But I overcame the countless obstacles in my path and pushed forward to get what I knew deep down I really deserved in life. My hope is that in reading my story you are inspired. That you begin to realise that *anything* is possible; that if you aspire to be incredible with women, you really can be.

In reading my story you will see the challenges I faced and how I dealt with them. This will provide you with a map to navigate the sometimes-stormy seas of personal transformation and the path to a newfound confidence and success with women. You will be equipped with a perspective that I simply did not have, and this will allow you to greatly accelerate the pace at which you improve with women. It took me years to get where I am today. For many of my students it takes just weeks and, in some cases, just days.

In the second chapter, titled 'The Attraction', you will learn what attraction really is, how it works and, most importantly, how to be a guy who makes women feel it. If you're thinking that it has something to do with having fantastic facial features or a big bank account, I suspect you will be pleasantly surprised. The truth is, there are a few 'triggers' that cause attraction in women. In this section, you will learn them, and the result will be responses from women that far surpass anything you've ever experienced before. Women will attempt to lock eyes with you when you pass them walking down the street, they'll laugh at your jokes even when you're not funny and they'll generally make the whole process of seduction *very* easy for you.

In 'The Seduction' you will learn the exact steps you need to take in order to seduce a woman in a smooth, natural fashion. We'll begin with the overarching structure of a seduction that I have developed – the 'three characters of seduction' model – and then in subsequent chapters we'll go step by step through the model, giving you all the methods and techniques you will need to make it work.

This includes how to approach a woman whom you've just laid eyes on; what to say to her to immediately lower her guard; how to build trust, comfort and a deep connection; how to smoothly take things forward in a sexual way, while limiting any chance of rejection that might have existed; and how to handle the days and weeks following your first encounter so that you maintain control of the relationship, whether you want it to be a casual thing or something more serious.

We will then turn our attention to specific situations, such as meeting women during the daytime, online dating and a whole host of situations in which you may find yourself at one point or another. With the information contained in these chapters, you can easily master the skills and become a natural at dealing comfortably and effectively with women.

A Word of Caution

When you have completed this book, you will possess a kind of raw power that at first can be intoxicating. With great power comes great responsibility. I encourage you to use your moral compass when operating from this new place of strength. Use these skills to treat women better, not worse. And when you find that special someone, offer her the love and respect she deserves.

1. From Geek to Natural

Wherever you are right now with women, I promise you that my situation was worse.

I entered this world on 7 July 1980 – in one of the slummiest and most dangerous parts of London, where I was born to a struggling young single mother who raised me the best way that she knew how. My father, who I hear is an actor somewhere in Italy, dumped us both before I even arrived. I grew up pretty much scared shitless, shy and geeky … a natural-born loser and outcast from the very start.

Deathly insecure, I was a total failure when it came to any and all social interactions from primary school on to well past university. It's hard to believe now, but up until I was twenty-one, I had never even gone on a single date, much less kissed a girl. Back then, if you'd looked up the word 'geek' in the dictionary, you probably would have found a picture of me.

Sad but true.

Growing up poor and paralysed by fear and insecurity, I was so shy and messed up that I couldn't even answer the phone or make a call to order a pizza! Needless to say, I kept pretty much to myself. When I wasn't at school being picked on or bullied, I played solitary video games for hours on end in our tiny council flat in Battersea, or at my eccentric grandmother's house nearby, while my mother worked as a telephonist at BT.

In short, I was a total mess.

- ✓ I was the kid at the neighbourhood birthday parties and other gatherings that everyone always asked, 'What's wrong?' or 'Are you okay?' Meeting new people terrified me, so I avoided it at all costs. I was nervous, shy and socially inept. As a result, I often annoyed people by saying the wrong things at the wrong times. I was hopeless.

- ✓ Plagued by low self-esteem and with no dad in the house to teach me how to fight back, I was constantly bullied by classmates who called me names like 'Big Head' and 'Moley' – the latter because of the birthmarks that I still have on my face.

- ✓ I have no doubt that I was clinically depressed for much of the time, even well past secondary school. With few friends, I hung around mostly with my cousin Alistair, who was five years younger than me but miles ahead in the maturity department.

On the rare occasion that I was invited by a classmate or neighbour to attend a party or do something, I would always find a reason not to. 'I'm sick' or 'I have too much homework' were my standard excuses. But deep down inside I was dying to be popular. And the older I got, the more desperate I became. I worried myself to sleep every night wondering if I would ever in my life have a girlfriend.

Here's a classic example of how screwed up I was as a teenager. By some magical fluke (or probably more like a delusion in my own mind), when I was sixteen there was a nice girl in my class who I could tell sort of liked me. I spent that whole year fantasising about her and trying to work up the nerve to say something – anything – to her, but I just couldn't do it. After months of trying, the best I could manage was to leave a handwritten note on her bike saying that I liked her and that we should go out on a date sometime. Needless to say, that approach didn't work, and she pretty much hid from me for the rest of the term.

After finishing from secondary school a total virgin – in fact, a guy who had never even held a girl's hand, much less kissed a girl or gone out on a date – I entered a crummy little university because it was the only one that would accept me. My grades were as bad as my social skills: I'd regularly skipped classes all through school because I was bullied so much, so I was always behind.

Nevertheless, I decided I wanted to study to become a schoolteacher. Year 1, to be precise. At least *those* kids wouldn't pick on me, I reasoned – plus the coursework would be easy. Mostly, though, I wanted to go to uni to try to socialise and to get a girlfriend. But, boy, were my attempts pathetic.

One night that first year, I ran into a girl who lived in my hall. She was stumbling down the hallway, obviously more than a little drunk, when she came over to me and said, 'Hey, Richard. I'm … really horny!' My God, she was gorgeous. Even hammered, she was irresistible. So how did I handle this sensational opportunity? Why, in the wimpiest way I could, of course. I said, 'Oh, dear,' patted her on the arm, and made a stupid excuse about needing to go somewhere – and then I ran out of the building as fast as I could. Afterwards, I didn't even have much regret. I didn't know how to kiss, after all – never mind how to take things to a sexual level. The next time I saw her, she had a bemused look on her face. Sometime later she said that she thought I must have been a virgin. Bingo!

Around that same time, I was on the street one day when two super-hot female students around my age came over to me. One of them said, 'Hey, you look a lot like my ex-boyfriend.' Just like before, all I could do was smile and say, 'Oh, really?' before rushing right past them. Yet again, I let an opportunity to score evaporate into thin air.

A few months later, I was on a train when a group of girls started talking to me. One of them, giggling, asked if I'd ever had a threesome. 'Wow,' I thought to myself, 'this is my lucky day.' Not! You guessed it. Before I could work up the courage to ask for their names and their phone numbers, they got off at the next stop.

The bottom line is that overtly sexual girls scared the hell out of me, because I was clueless about how to handle them. This was never more evident than the night I was out at my local pub when an attractive young woman came up to me and said, 'Would you like to lick my lizard?' I was like, 'What?!' She then proceeded to show me a small lizard tattoo that she had on her belly. Shockingly, I managed to respond properly (that is, to respond *at all*) and I gave her lizard a quick lick. She stood there expectantly. As my mind raced through various potential comebacks, I said absolutely nothing. And so she left.

That was me – back when I had no cool. When I had no confidence. When I had no game whatsoever – natural, learned or self-taught. It's not like opportunities weren't presenting themselves, because they certainly were. It was that I had no fucking idea how to recognise or respond to them.

I was a man without skills, tools, techniques or tips on how to succeed with the opposite sex. To make matters worse, I ended up failing that first year of university. Clearly, I was due for a change.

So I dropped out of uni, moved back in with my mum, and took a temporary job as a marketing assistant at a local software company. My primary duties were doing odd jobs and 'gofer' work to help my bosses get their big presentations together. Easy stuff. I also tracked the daily stock market performance of the company's main competitors. Although this was a small part of my job, I soon discovered it was the bit I liked the most.

During this time, I was pretty much a total recluse when I wasn't working. I never went out at night. All I did was work, eat, play video games in my room and sleep. I also saved my money and started studying the stock market.

Since my mum didn't charge me for room or board, after a few months I'd saved up a couple of thousand pounds from working. I asked a friend of my mum's, who dabbled in the stock market herself, to invest it for me. I had a hunch and had her pursue it for me. I got lucky and that stock went up ... about tenfold. This gave me the confidence to quit my job and try my hand as a personal investor – a day trader – working from home. I got lucky once and thought I'd be the next Warren Buffett. While that didn't happen, I did manage to stay afloat and not lose money. Some years I was up, others I was down, but I generally did quite well, given my poor track record in life. While a small bit of success was a divergence from my past, one thing definitely did not change: I was still scared shitless of socialising. When I look back now, I realise that the reason I spent so much time at my computer, trading stocks, was so that I could hide from the reality that I was so poor socially. With every click of the mouse and with every financial transaction, I got to feel important instead of incompetent and ashamed of myself. I can't remember ever, during my years as a trader, leaving my house at night to meet women. I'd tried that before, in university, and it didn't work. I was terrified to fail again.

One night, when I was twenty-one years old, I went to sleep with tears running down my cheeks. I'd spent all this time chasing money as a trader, and for the first time I realised that I was just doing everything I could to avoid the pain of being a pariah yet again. What I *really* wanted was a girlfriend. I wanted to be loved. I wanted to experience what it seemed like everyone else took for granted. And as I finally went to sleep that night, I told myself I'd give up everything I had to find that one special girl.

———

A few nights later I uncharacteristically agreed to go out to a nightclub with one of the few male friends that I had. This, in itself, was a huge accomplishment for me. Soon enough, he clicked with a hot-looking chick who happened to have a rather nice-looking friend with her. Because she and I were left to fend for ourselves, we had no choice but to talk to each other while our friends were off having a great time on the dance floor. I was nervous and couldn't hold good eye contact, but I guess she liked my nice-guy mild manner. Meanwhile, my friend and the other girl were getting along so well that he wanted to take her back to his place. He offered to drop us off at our homes on the way, so we went to 'my' girl's street first. Everyone said goodbye, and she got out of the car.

As she walked the first few steps towards her front door, I sat in the back – paralysed – gripping the seat beneath me for all it was worth. That's when it happened: I had one of those life-changing moments when you force yourself to take action.

Asking my friend to wait, I lurched out of the car and ran after her. I called her name; she turned and I said, 'Can I have your number?' She shouted it out with a smile. This was the first time I'd ever got a girl's number in my life.

The next day, I didn't call because I was too nervous.

I called her the day after that, though. She didn't answer, but I managed to stutter out a brief message.

Heartbroken, I was certain that she had much better things to do than to speak to a loser like me. Amazingly, she called me back a couple of hours later after she got home from work. We arranged to meet for drinks a couple of days later. Things went pretty well, actually. It was my first date ever. We took it slow. I was psyched.

On our second date, I cooked dinner for her – another first! – at my place. Afterwards, she sat next to me on the sofa, put her head on my shoulder, and ... I stroked her hair!

On the third date, we finally had our (and my) first kiss – with her making the first move, of course. My bliss was short-lived, because as soon as the kiss was over she promptly informed me that she had a boyfriend. Luckily for me, she also said that the relationship wasn't really working. But then she dropped another bombshell, saying that she was planning to start university soon at a place that was more than four hours away.

'Hey, no problem,' I assured her, even though we had only kissed. 'I'll book a hotel room and visit you every weekend.'

We spent the next two and a half years together. The relationship went about as well as you might imagine: I was both very needy and very inexperienced. During that whole time I had this nagging feeling that I was stuck in the relationship because it was the only one I could get. And even though I was thankful for the chance to be with a girl, somehow it seemed like I was missing out on something. Eventually, we began arguing and things deteriorated until we broke up.

Back to square one for me. Only now I was twenty-three years old, suddenly single and still living at home with my mother. Out of sheer desperation, and not knowing what to do with my life, I began working on myself – just trying to improve, to do whatever it took not to be so bad at life. I wanted to be so much more than I had been up to that point.

I started by writing down all my problems, all the ways in which I wanted to be better; and then I made up a plan for addressing each one. For my shyness, for example, I decided to do a TEFL (Teaching English as a Foreign Language) course in Seville, Spain. It forced me, as I hoped it would when I first read the prospectus, to be the centre of attention and stand up in front of a class of people for an hour at a time. In my first class, I was so nervous that my voice was shaking. By the last one though, I was pretty good. Much of getting over shyness, and even fear, in approaching women relies on desensitisation. That course really helped me a lot.

I also started reading two self-improvement books a week. I studied neurolinguistic programming (NLP), which is a branch of psychology that uses different techniques, such as the artful use of language and visualisation to influence not only one's own subconscious mind but also the subconscious minds of others. I also studied mainstream psychology, hypnosis, Buddhism and other self-development approaches. I didn't anticipate the effect this would have, but it made me calmer and more composed, and generally happier and more contented. Buddhism and hypnosis made my focus of attention internal.

My clothes also needed fixing, and I spent a period of about two years trying to figure out what worked best for me in terms of my style. I went from wearing baggy jeans, Nike tops and dirty running shoes to well-fitting, stylish designer clothes that I bought at discount outlets. At first, I made mistakes and bought terrible items (the fake Versace polo shirt with a huge logo, the Zegna suit that was two sizes too big), but over time I refined my style and learned a lot about labels, design, fit and fabrics – and where to shop for the best bargains.

I still wasn't dating, but I was getting ready. And soon enough, fate would accidentally step into the picture.

I was sitting at a Starbucks with my cousin and confidant, Alistair, listening to music on my iPod, when I noticed a bunch of geeky-looking guys about my age sitting nearby. They were listening intently to what another man at their table was telling them. They looked like they were taking a class.

Intrigued, I pulled out my earphones and leaned over to try to eavesdrop. From what I could hear, it sounded like they were taking notes about how to pick up girls.

'Hey, you! Over there!' the man who was doing the talking suddenly shouted out in my direction. 'You better not be taping me!'

Alistair and I quickly explained that my iPod wasn't a tape recorder, and with that the man's face softened and he invited us over to his table. That's when I first learned about the world of the pickup artist, or PUA. He explained that he was a PUA coach and that the guys with him were his students. I was intrigued. He told me to go out and buy a book called *The Game* by some American guy named Neil Strauss. He said I should read it and, if I liked what I read, I might want to give him a call and sign up for his class.

From looking at the guys who were with him, though, I didn't really buy into the idea that they could have any success with women – they just looked too plain geeky. Even my teenage cousin and I were a lot hipper and cooler than they were, which isn't saying a lot.

Nevertheless, I asked young Alistair to run over to the nearby Borders bookshop to check out the book. An hour later, he called me from the store. 'Hey, Rich! I've found it! It's great!' he said excitedly. 'It's by a journalist who infiltrated this underground society of pickup artists.' He said it wasn't so great in terms of offering actual tips and techniques, but he liked what he'd read. I said, 'Buy it!'

I read the entire book that night – cover to cover – in one sitting. I never signed up for a class, but I did spend the next six months devouring everything I could get my hands on (via the Internet) about the guys who were featured in the book. Guys like Mystery and David DeAngelo. I diligently studied the subject on my own, learning the techniques, memorising the lines. Eventually, I decided to start trying it out for myself. After successfully pulling off ten small 'approaches' (starting brief conversations with a new woman), I felt I was finally beginning to get the hang of it.

Shortly after studying *The Game*, I went to Singapore on holiday. I was visiting my ex-girlfriend, whom I still had feelings for but was no longer in love with. She did, however, have a colleague I was attracted to. I was there for a month and bumped into this girl a few times. She had been educated at Oxford, and I loved her Liz Hurley accent. One night, when we were in a bar and she was sitting next to me, I put a small amount of my 'learning' to use.

She put her hand on my leg, so I put *my* hand on *her* leg. She started rubbing my leg, so I reciprocated. She took my hand, so I leaned in and kissed her.

I would have been happy with just a kiss, this being only the second girl I'd kissed in my entire life! However, she escalated things further. 'Let's go,' she said, leading me outside to a cab and back to my hotel. Truth be told, she did all the work. In the hotel room, she took her clothes off, lay back and made my job as easy as it could possibly be. I was finally getting somewhere!

My confidence was already boosted from all the pickup artist theory now stored in my head. I felt I had a secret weapon I could deploy with devastating results. And why not? It had a 100 per cent success rate so far. Other guys didn't know this stuff. They were idiots! I was going to clean up! Okay, so she was the one who said, 'Let's go', who got us in a cab and took us back to a hotel; and she was a friend of a friend, rather than a cold approach – but, hey!, I'd got the result, and now I was determined to get even better at dealing with women.

A few months later, I moved out of my mother's place and into a flatshare in a cool part of London. I picked the location specifically for meeting women, going out and being sociable. I didn't know anyone – not even my flat-mates – so I knew I'd be forced to get out there and meet people.

Being new to the neighbourhood, I had no immediate social circle to connect with or to hang out with, so I eventually linked up with some local pickup artists via online forums and I started to tag along with them when they went out on the town.

When we first went out I gave them the same kind of respect I'd given to the master pickup artists described in *The Game*. I thought that anyone who had spent years working on something would be very good at it. However, I quickly found out that most of these guys could talk a good talk and walk a cool walk, but they didn't seem to have a clue about how to take things much further than getting a girl's phone number, a first dance or a kiss.

I'd watch one of those guys approach and see the girls look at each other with a 'Help me!' face, or I'd see them simply smile politely, shake their heads and say, 'What was up with that guy?' after he turned his back. To me, it was kind of sad, and I knew that I wanted more.

Luckily, I had some other role models that I could admire (on video and audio at least), but I still began to question the full potential of all the touted strategies. If these guys had taken years of focused effort just to get where they were – which wasn't far, in my book – maybe I'd never be able to become what I really wanted to be, which was a genuinely successful seducer who knew how to attract and handle beautiful women.

Quite frankly, I wasn't interested in just scoring 'bragging rights' about quick little victories such as getting a good-looking girl's phone number or a quick kiss on the dance floor. I wanted more. I wanted to be the coolest guy in the room, the guy that gets the girl *and* also has of bunch of cool friends and a social life.

Bottom line: I wanted it all. I wanted to be the real deal.

Needless to say, I had to reevaluate my motives and my expectations. I realised pretty quickly that my goal should be to 'game' not like a typical pickup artist but like a 'natural' – someone who exudes the qualities a woman would naturally be attracted to … someone who doesn't need tricks and gimmicks or lies to make women fall for him.

Over the next few weeks, I met more of the same kind of guys – pickup artist wannabes who hadn't yet mastered the game. Most of them I didn't really want to hang out with, but I did meet two, Eugene and Conor, who were cooler than the others, and I tried to go out to as many bars and clubs with them as I could. At this point, unless I'd gone to a particular club or bar more than thirty times – which is a lot! – I still felt fairly uncomfortable with the environment.

Little by little, however, I was beginning to overcome my fear of talking to women, and a couple of times I even

had some nice conversations, thanks to my inherent intro-
vert skill of being a good listener. Eventually, with the help
of Conor as my 'wingman', or social accomplice, I was able
to get a few phone numbers in various clubs, but nothing
came of them.

For example, one girl I was sure I'd meet for a date –
after we'd had a great conversation, I took her number and
we arranged to meet the next week at a salsa club – but
she texted me to say she'd hurt her ankle at the gym. After
that, I tried to meet up with her a few times, but it never
happened; she always had an excuse. My education and
practice in attracting women continued.

The next big realisation happened several weeks later,
when I was at a club with Conor. He approached two
very attractive Swedish girls and seemed to settle on one.
I waited a short while and then joined them. Conor was
totally focused on his girl, but I wasn't having much luck
with her friend. After sitting on the arm of her chair for
a full hour, talking to her, and then finally finding a way
to sit down next to her, I felt like I was getting absolutely
nowhere.

I was getting no touching from her, and didn't know
what the hell I should do. My previous one-night stand in
Singapore had happened only because the girl had touched
my leg first; I'd just matched her moves with a few of my
own. Frustrated now, I said to myself, 'Fuck it,' put my
arm around the Swedish girl, and went in for the kiss. Lo
and behold, it worked! She was into it!

Now I know I probably could have made that move after
thirty seconds rather than waiting a whole hour, and I
probably could have moved on from the kiss to something
more, but the point is that taking the initiative shifted

something in my mind. I realised that women like men to lead; asking a woman if she wants to kiss, or waiting ages to do it, is just unattractive. In this case I didn't have the knowledge I have now, so I could have been rejected when I went for it – but if you don't try, you won't ever find out what you might have missed. (I should note here that lunging in suddenly for a kiss is a terrible thing to do. When you read the later chapters in this book, you'll learn the way to do it smoothly.)

The next milestone happened one night when I was at a trendy dance club. The friend I was with identified a hot girl. She was tall, blonde and thin, with blue eyes – just my type. I went over and sat down next to her and started chatting away. After some teasing banter to challenge her, I lightly touched her leg and arm, and she reciprocated. I went for the kiss after about five minutes. Then I led her around the club: 'Let's go get a drink' became 'Let's dance,' which then became 'Let's sit down.' We got quite hot and heavy on the sidelines, and then I just got up, took her hand and said, 'Let's go.' She walked with me, asking only, 'Where?' I said, 'Somewhere else,' and led her out of the club and over to my place.

An hour later we were in bed. She left early in the morning to get back home, and I was buzzing. My God! I'd finally scored with an attractive girl – a perfect stranger – and within a matter of hours had persuaded her that I was good enough for her to sleep with. I was on my way.

———

In the days, weeks and months that followed, I worked furiously on my game. Now that I'd got a little taste of success, I was a man on a mission: to get as good at the pickup game as humanly possible. Night after night I went out and put into practice everything that I'd learned. Lots of what I tried didn't work. But every now and again I'd come up with a new twist on an old technique, and when it worked I'd incorporate it into my skill set. As my game evolved, I became very, very good – a natural, or so it appeared. So good, in fact, that it was upsetting the people I used to go out with. While my wingmen would be prowling the club to make their first approach, I'd be making out with a girl in the corner of the club. I moved on to sleeping with strippers. Then came models and actresses. All the while my confidence and skill grew.

While some of my old wingmen were mad that I'd become so good, others began to approach me for help. They realised that although I had started 'gaming' long after they did, my progress was much faster. And while everyone talked a good game, I was the only man in my original circle of friends who was consistently sleeping with women who were hot enough to be on TV and in magazines.

For the first few months I trained guys one on one, giving them lessons 'in the field'. In other words, I would take them out with me and basically show them what I was doing. They'd ask questions and I'd answer and then demonstrate. Wash, rinse and repeat. Soon my students were getting results just as good as I was getting, and I realised that what I had was a skill set that could be shared and taught. Eager to get the word out to more people about what I had developed, and to help guys who were in the position I'd been in when I began, I started a website, puatraining.com, and offered my first ever seduction 'bootcamp'.

PUA Training was born.

Since then it's been a wild, wacky ride. I've trained thousands of 'students' personally, released multiple bestselling DVD training sets, been on just about every television station you can imagine and been spotted and spoken to by students all over the world.

Whether I'm in New York, Buenos Aires or Hong Kong, students recognise me on the streets and come up to me, thanking me for the information I've shared, often telling me about the results they've got using my teachings. I have to tell you, nothing is more humbling. The opportunity to change lives is what drives me, and these last few years have been an absolute blessing.

My goal in writing this book, the one you are about to read, is to impact on yet another life: yours. My hope is that you draw inspiration from my own personal journey and then use what you're about to learn to write your own.

2. The Attraction

We've all seen it: the overweight man in his midfifties with a beautiful twenty-something on his arm, the less-than-good-looking guy who never shows up at a party without a few models, the unemployed car mechanic who practically has a waiting line at his bedroom door.

The generally accepted beliefs about what makes a man attractive would dictate that these situations couldn't occur. But they do. And they're more common than most people realise.

How is this possible?

Simple: the generally accepted view of how attraction works ... is *wrong*.

The Truth About Attraction: Status Matters

Yes, it's true that we guys are attracted to beautiful, young women.

But women? They want something entirely different. They want a *man* – but not just any man. They want one who is confident, powerful, socially savvy and high in status.

The reason for this is rooted in evolutionary biology.

Over thousands of years men and women developed preferences for sexual partners based on criteria that allowed for the successful rearing of future generations. While men evolved the desire for women with big breasts, clear skin and beautiful smiles – signs of fertility and health that would increase the likelihood of successful childrearing – women evolved differently: they developed a preference for men who would be able to protect their offspring and provide for them in an often dangerous and uncertain world.

Because of the tribal context in which this development occurred, women evolved to feel attraction for men at the top of the social totem pole – in other words, men of high status.

So what exactly *is* status? Well, in any group of men, there is a hierarchal formation, and a man's status is where he falls in that ranking. On top is the leader – the alpha male, to borrow a term from scientists who study the animal world. He is the person in the group who is the most important. He is the one who exhibits the most influence upon others. He is the one who calls the shots.

Being the leader is not an easy job. He has to make tough decisions, not only for himself but for the group as a whole, and he must shoulder the responsibility of whatever happens as a result of his decisions and actions. The rewards are plentiful, though: he gets first pick of available resources – and this includes women.

To trigger a social response in women, we've got to let them know that we are this special type of high-status male. Our job would be incredibly easy if we could just say, 'Hey, I'm the leader!' or 'Hey, I'm an alpha male!' But as I'm sure you know, this simply doesn't work.

In the absence of that sort of explicit statement, women who want to determine what kind of man you are instead watch your behaviour, looking for subtle cues that indicate where you stand in this world. Thus, to become attractive, you must examine the behaviour of highly attractive males and then demonstrate it yourself. Men who do this become very attractive to women.

It's important here for me to address something head-on: what I'm talking about right now is not pretending to be someone you aren't in order to 'trick' women. Instead, this is about using an understanding of human behaviour, psychology and biology to consciously change the ways in which you act to become a more powerful, confident and attractive version of who you already are.

Modelling 'Alpha'

How does the alpha male behave? How does he think? What makes him so different from the beta males? These were the questions I began asking myself as I embarked on my own transformation from lowly geek to master lothario.

For months I pored over scientific literature, watched movies with powerful male leads and observed social interactions across a variety of settings, all with a pen and paper in hand, furiously taking notes.

Ultimately, I arrived at a set of five characteristics present in nearly all high-status males and conspicuously absent in most low-status males.

These traits are:

1. A strong sense of self-belief

2. A strong physical presence

3. The ability and willingness to lead and make decisions

4. A cool, calm and collected demeanour in high-pressure situations

5. Social intelligence (the ability to connect and communicate with others)

After determining that these were the 'alpha traits' I'd been looking for, I spent the following days, weeks and months developing methods and techniques for changing the way I thought, felt and behaved so that I could embody these traits myself and finally become the cool, attractive guy I'd always wanted to be.

I'm happy to report that I was *very* successful in doing this. In fact, as you've just read in earlier pages, my transformation was nothing short of incredible.

What I'd like to do now is explain to you in a bit more depth what each of the five alpha traits is, how they all work and, most importantly, the path you can take to acquire them for yourself.

Let's begin with …

Alpha Trait No.1:
A Strong Sense of Self-Belief

An attractive man is one who has a very strong sense of self: a man who likes himself, trusts himself and is confident in his own ability to act effectively in the world. At the root of his psychology is a strong set of beliefs – about himself, about how other people should treat him and about what he is entitled to. These beliefs empower him to behave in an attractive manner and get what he wants in life. This includes women.

Why are a man's beliefs so essential to his success with women?

The answer is that our beliefs shape our behaviours. And our behaviours dictate how others perceive us and treat us.

If you hold a deep conviction that you are a force of nature – an attractive man whom women can't keep their hands off – you will start to behave in attractive new ways.

Women will pick up on your behaviour, determine that you are a man with a strong sense of self and thus begin to feel attracted to you.

If this sounds a little 'woo-woo' to you, I promise you, it's not.

For the first twenty-three years of my life I had a very low sense of self. I thought I was ugly. I thought I was an outsider. I thought women wanted nothing to do with me. And because I thought these things, I behaved in a way that communicated to others, 'Hey, I'm not very important, so please don't treat me well!'

When I began working on my beliefs, actively changing them to new and more empowering ones, everything began to change. Women even began telling me I was good-looking – something that had never happened before.

So how can you change your beliefs? I recommend an integrated approach. By this I mean working on your belief system directly, through the two exercises that I'm about to show you – using affirmations and putting yourself in 'the zone' – and also indirectly, by going out into the real world and applying the seduction skills that I will teach you in the latter part of this book. Neither approaching women nor doing 'inner game' exercises will transform your beliefs on their own. But when you combine the two, the rate at which your whole reality begins to transform will astonish you.

Affirming Your Worth

I recommend a special twist on the well-known tool known as affirmations. As you may know, affirmations are positive statements you make about yourself that act on your subconscious mind. Over time they affect your self-image, confidence and beliefs. Want to test their effectiveness before committing? Write a list of all the things you like about yourself on one side of a piece of paper. Then, on the other side, write out all of the things that you don't like. Notice how your mood is affected differently when you read each side. By writing and then using positive affirmations, you counteract the generally negative influences that other people, the media and society have on your self-esteem and belief system.

Keep your list of positive affirmations about yourself in a notebook by your bed. Read them as frequently as you can. Something else that I did – and really benefited from – was to record my self-affirmations onto an MP3 player and play them on a low-volume loop for hours. This strategy allows the positive beliefs to sink deep into your subconscious mind while your conscious mind is distracted by day-to-day things.

Here are the rules for making affirmations work:

1. They should be positive statements written in the present tense: 'I am friendly', not 'I will be friendly'.

2. They should avoid negative words: 'I'm not an idiot' should be 'I'm clever'. 'I don't get rejected' should be 'All women love me'. The subconscious doesn't understand negatives. Imagine if someone told you *not* to think about a pink elephant. What would happen? You'd think of a pink elephant. So saying, 'I'm not a loser who gets rejected and everyone hates,' is just as bad as saying, 'I *am* a loser who gets rejected and everyone hates.'

3. They should be based on how you picture your ideal self – the person you'd like to be, you at your best.

4. They should make you feel something when you say them. If you write an affirmation and it doesn't have that effect, change the language around or scrap it altogether.

You can write affirmations as individual statements or in paragraph form. However you choose to present them, they *will* change your life. I wrote my first affirmations in mid-2003, and they all came true within a couple of years.

It's spooky how it happened. At the time they seemed outside the realm of possibility, but my subconscious helped me make them a reality. I urge you, please don't write these off as silly. They work.

Below are some examples of affirmations you can use. However, please be sure to make yours meaningful to *you*.

✓ I am a leader.

✓ I am interesting.

✓ I am a success in all that I do.

✓ I can attract any woman I want.

✓ I know my purpose.

✓ I am confident in who I am.

✓ I am cool, calm and collected.

✓ I am charismatic.

✓ My world and my life are attractive and interesting.

✓ People meet me and want to know me.

✓ I am interested in other people.

✓ I meet fun, positive people.

Putting Yourself in 'The Zone'

How you act is not determined by just your beliefs; it's also influenced by your 'state', or your feelings of resourcefulness and power. Have you ever been 'in the zone'? Perhaps it was at your job, or possibly with a women. Regardless of the specific situation, you felt like you could do anything you wanted and it would just work: that's what being 'in state' or 'in the zone' is all about. When you're 'out of state', 'out' of the zone, you struggle to do the things that you can easily do when you're empowered. When I was improving my life with women, being out of state really frustrated me. To counter that frustration, I developed a technique for rapidly putting myself in the zone – that is, triggering that frame of mind where I feel like I can conquer the world.

Here's how to do it:

Got your affirmations from before? Great. Now pick out a handful of songs that have extremely positive associations for you – songs that really get you going. Start playing those songs loudly and really get into them, allowing yourself to experience a strong, positive emotional state. Then, once you've got that positive emotion coursing through your body, begin emphatically saying your affirmations. At the same time, snap your fingers and get your body moving to generate some energy.

After you've repeated this little ritual about five to seven times, the music, the affirmations and the emotions will all begin to associate with one another. Then, when you want to feel confident and in the zone, all you need to do

State Control Toolkit

✓ Small MP3 player for taking your music (and recorded affirmations) anywhere.

✓ A sheet of paper with written affirmations.

✓ A definitive body movement such as finger-snapping.

is say an affirmation or two, snap your fingers or listen to one of the songs you have chosen for your state-building exercise – and voilà: you're there.

When you're in state, in the zone, you feel confident. You feel attractive. You feel like the most powerful person in the room. This deep emotional conviction will radiate from you, and other people will feel your power. The men will follow your lead. The women will become attracted to you.

These two exercises should put you on the path towards mastering your beliefs and your state. When you couple them with the actual approaching you will be doing after you learn the seduction techniques in the latter part of the book, you will begin to experience rapid and dramatic changes.

Alpha Trait No.2: A Strong Physical Presence

High-status men have different body language from that of the typical male. Every man, whether alpha or beta, gives off clear nonverbal indicators to women of their rank and their level of attractiveness. Let's first look at how most men carry themselves, and then we'll focus on how to display the body language of a powerful male in order to increase our attraction to and interest from women.

Low-Status Body Language

Most men fidget. They're nervous, and it shows. Their weight shifts from leg to leg. When they're out at a bar, they hold their drinks up close to their chest and frequently take sips. They don't take up much physical space, literally.

And that's when they're by themselves. When they talk to women and other men, it gets worse: they're afraid to touch, gesture or show much expression – on top of the nervous movements described above.

All of the above are nonverbal signs of low status.

High-Status Body Language

In order to stand out from 99 per cent of guys out there and establish yourself as a confident and powerful man, follow these guidelines:

✓ *Legs.* Stand with your feet slightly wider apart than is natural. It will feel strange at first, but you'll also feel completely rooted, like a tree. This will stop you from changing position or shifting your weight.

✓ *Arms.* Most people I train have a problem with fidgeting; they move their hands around, play with their cuffs or watch, touch their face, put their hands in their pockets and out again, and just can't stay still. This is a sign of insecurity, and women will pick up on it immediately. Here's a trick to get over this: put your thumb against your index and middle fingers and let your hands fall to your sides. This removes the natural tendency for the fingers to find something to do. You can stay in this position comfortably for hours without moving.

✓ *Eyes.* Don't look down! It conveys weakness. Be confident; hold eye contact with people. But remember, it isn't a staring match; soft, natural eye contact is what you need. If you need some time to

become confident holding eye contact and still feel
the need to look away, break eye contact to the side
rather than down.

✓ *Head*. Move your head slowly – that conveys high
status. Quick head movements make you look
nervous.

✓ *Space*. Take up lots of space. *Own* the room! When
sitting, spread yourself out. When standing, have
a wide, confident stance or use gestures. When
dancing, move around the dance floor a lot and
use big arm movements (though be careful not to
knock people over). In the past, I always used to
get barged out of the way and my toes trodden on;
since I started using alpha body language, people
give me more space and this never happens. You'll
know you're doing things right when the same
happens to you.

I cannot overstate the importance of adopting the
correct body language. Because so many guys get it wrong,

Assignment No.1

Practise the alpha stance in your home to see how it
looks in the mirror. Next time you're in a bar, observe
other people's body language based on the guidelines
above. See who has good and bad body language. Be
very aware of your own and try to switch into alpha body
language as often and as fast as possible.

when you fix yours you'll stand out from the pack in a major way and women will notice.

At first it might be a little difficult to alter the way you carry yourself. That's perfectly okay. Breaking old habits is a process of first becoming aware of what you're doing wrong; then noticing when you're doing it, stopping it and eventually replacing this behaviour.

One of the major benefits of our live PUA Training programmes is that we can observe students' nonverbal communication and can instantly identify and correct things that most people just wouldn't pick up on – things like nervous tics or awkward mannerisms – all things that are unattractive. Trust me, we've all had them. I used to laugh nervously and touch my face. It took my brutally honest cousin (who was also studying pickup techniques) to point this out.

Alpha Trait No.3:
The Ability and Willingness to
Lead and Make Decisions

Alpha males make decisions, both for themselves and for the groups that they lead. Whether it's something as trivial as where the group should eat dinner or something as serious as determining whether one group member needs to be ostracised, the alpha male is the one who makes the decisions.

Taking ownership of decisions is something that is not naturally comfortable for most people. There is, in many cases, a high risk of failure and negative ramifications. Because of this, when you can make decisions for a group, you are in effect 'stepping up'.

You are doing the tough job, and because of this people will respect you. The more people respect you, the more power and authority you will be granted. And the more power you have, the more you can influence and lead.

Using the Power of Certainty

There is a little loophole in human psychology: whoever is most certain wins. In other words, when multiple people have multiple ideas or viewpoints, the person who believes most certainly that he or she is correct will generally win out and influence others. Those who have relatively little in the way of an opinion will look to the person who is most certain to make decisions for them.

Just realising this one simple fact makes a world of difference. Approach the world with the idea that 'whoever is most certain wins' and you will find that you get very different results.

When it's lunchtime and your friends start grumbling about being hungry, make a decision. Say 'Let's go here' or 'Let's go there' with absolute certainty. Don't ask if this is okay with everyone. Just assume it is – and it will be.

(Additional tip: if you want to make your statement more persuasive, add the word 'because' and then just about any reason, and people will even more readily comply with your suggestion – for example, 'Let's go to that place around the corner because they have the best burgers.')

Start small. Begin practicing decisiveness and leadership when you and your friends are deciding where to have lunch. Then, as you get more comfortable and confident with the process, begin stepping up in increasingly more pressure-filled situations. Before long, you will have established yourself as a natural leader in your group – and a dominant personality in every interaction you have.

Women will take notice, and their attraction to you will increase.

Holding Your Power with Beautiful Women

Just as you must hold your power with the men around you, you must exercise it when in the presence of women as well. The more beautiful the woman, the more she's used to being given all the status. A deferential man will ask her to make decisions on everything, from whether it's okay to take her phone number and when she's available to meet, to where she would like to go, whether his clothes are okay and if the food at a proposed restaurant is good. This is actually very unattractive. It's so common for men to give away all their power like this that the rare man who *doesn't* is prized.

The rules for maintaining status when dealing with a woman are simple:

1. Don't ask lots of questions when you're facing a decision together.

2. Don't give her the decision-making power. Only give her the option to accept your choices. 'Where would you like to eat?' gives her the decision-making power, but 'Let's go to the Italian place?' gives her only the chance to go along with your decision.

3. Don't seek approval: 'Is this okay?', 'Is that all right with you?', 'How's my jacket look?'

4. Lead: 'I'm hungry; let's go eat,' or 'I'm thirsty; let's go get a drink.'

A perfect example of this high-status behaviour is Don Draper, a character in the series *Mad Men*. If you haven't seen him in action, I highly recommend that you get the DVDs and watch him. (Also, it's a great show.)

Alpha Trait No.4: A Cool, Calm and Collected Demeanour in High-Pressure Situations

If you were to observe a social situation from afar, you would likely notice that one person seemed significantly more comfortable and relaxed than the other(s). This level of comfort is a nonverbal sign of status and value and is something that, with a little bit of practice, you can absolutely achieve.

There are three types of comfort in particular that you will want to master.

The first is quite simple; it is...

1. Comfort in the Environment

Examples: Bartenders, DJs and bouncers are all known to do very well with women. The main reason for this is that they're the most comfortable guys in the place, because they're there every night and the environment can't faze them. But let's get something clear – most bartenders are not high-status guys. The other guys in the club could be millionaire businessmen wearing thousand-pound suits and buying bottles of exorbitantly expensive Cristal champagne. Bartenders, on the other hand, earn fairly low wages. It's purely that they look comfortable. There is no other secret to it.

How to get comfortable: The pickup environment that most betrays a lack of confidence at first glance is the nightclub. People don't often feel nervous when they're walking down the street or shopping, but in a club the pressure is so much more intense. This is even more of a problem with high-end venues. What needs to happen in this case is simple desensitisation. Pick a club and a day of the week to go there. Go with friends or on your own. Your mission is not to talk to anyone or do any gaming, but purely to become comfortable in the environment. Learn the layout; start to recognise familiar faces; have some casual conversations with staff.

The key is to get comfortable and start treating the place like your own home. Sit or stand comfortably in a low-energy, chilled-out way or genuinely enjoy the music, moving around without caring what others think or retreating into your head. Those are the only two effective modes of behaviour in the club; nothing in between will look comfortable. If you're trying to look like you enjoy the music by tapping a foot out of rhythm or nodding your head because you think you should, you won't look right. (Refer to the body language discussion earlier in this chapter for a fuller description.)

When you first enter a nightclub with the mission to become comfortable, be very observant; notice the guys who look comfortable and the ones who don't. Try to see things from the woman's point of view. By removing the pressure of needing to pick up or talk to women, you can start to enjoy the environment and create positive associations with it, rather than viewing it as a high-pressure place where you *must* game.

The second kind of comfort is ...

2. Comfort in Interacting with Beautiful Women

So, she's seen you and judged you as confident from a distance. As long as you don't make any mistakes with eye contact (breaking it downwards or generally being uncomfortable with it), you'll be fine all the way up to the actual approach. But how does a woman decide if you're a confident man when you're actually talking to her?

The next stage, then, is appearing comfortable in conversation. How could a beautiful girl ever be attracted to a man who isn't confident when interacting with her? Won't this make her feel uncomfortable in herself? (Okay, in maybe 2 per cent of cases she may think you're 'cute'. But 2 per cent of cases aren't any kind of game – apart from a numbers game.)

Examples: Guys who own a model agency, work in a strip club or manage a restaurant with hot waitresses all have something in common – they get laid. One of the major reasons is that they're desensitised to interacting with beautiful women and are therefore comfortable around them. Someone who has worked for a model agency for two years won't be shaking, sweating, breaking eye contact or looking generally nervous or uncomfortable if he meets a beautiful woman. She will recognise, consciously or unconsciously, that her beauty doesn't faze him, and this will mean he isn't viewed as a lower life form, unlike the other guys who are obviously very affected by her looks.

How to get comfortable: Go to places with a high concentration of very beautiful women, like exclusive department stores and high-end clubs, or visit major cities where stunning women populate the streets, like Moscow, Riga, Stockholm, Kiev and Rio (or countries such as Latvia, which has amazing women everywhere). In these situations set an achievable goal, which is simply to 'open' and leave. (We'll talk more about opening later.) Have your opener and your escape line ready – except in a strip club, where an opener isn't necessary since there the women open you. Desensitise yourself to their looks; get comfortable holding eye contact; learn to keep your composure. Through this experience you will realise that gorgeous women aren't so different or difficult to talk to, and they, for their part, will perceive you as comfortable, which will greatly increase your chances of building attraction.

The third and last type of comfort is …

3. Comfort in Your Own Skin

So you look confident from a distance (though most guys don't!). You seem confident when you're talking to her. What does she do then? She tests you out. She challenges you to see how you will react. She might ask you why you're wearing 'that jumper' if you are 'a player' or why you don't go to the gym. The test is to see if you are internally confident or comfortable in your own skin.

This testing is a good sign, because it starts to happen once she's becoming committed to the interaction and wants to find out if you're the man for her. This kind of testing will continue beyond those initial questions, and to measure up you will need to display various types of confidence, including physical escalation and sexual confidence.

Example: A guy who consistently goes with hot girls and is comfortable with who he is is nonreactive and unemotional in the face of tests. To get to this point, you have to put in a bit of work. I have a theory that people become shy because they're worried about exposing their weaknesses to others. They are scared of being perceived as ugly, or having a silly voice, or being poor, or whatever else. So they do little and say less so that they aren't found out. Someone who is content with himself will not be reticent to put himself out there and won't react as much if tested.

How to get comfortable: Sit down and write a list of your weak points, the things about yourself that you're not happy with. Next to each, write an action you can take to help it. That action might fix the issue by 100 per cent or maybe just 20 per cent, but having a plan for improving your situation, even just incrementally, will positively influence your confidence and self-esteem. Earlier in this book I talked about how I did this, and it was a massive factor in gaining the confidence I now possess. (Don't get me wrong – there are still aspects of myself that I'm not entirely satisfied with, but there are much fewer than there used to be.)

Alpha Trait No.5: Social Intelligence

High-status men have high levels of what is called 'social intelligence'. This is a term that encompasses many characteristics, but in general it describes an understanding and awareness of social dynamics and an ability to navigate them accordingly.

Becoming Socially Savvy

The primary component of social intelligence is the ability to connect and communicate with others – in other words, having basic social skills. A socially intelligent man knows how others around him feel at all times. He understands the status hierarchies, the power dynamics and the difference between cool and uncool.

Put simply, he's in the know, and, because of this, he comes off well in most company.

In the following chapters of this book, you will learn the dynamics of social situations and the skills you need to appropriately navigate any environment. When you master those skills, you will be seen as a man of high social intelligence, and this in itself will make you attractive.

The ability to walk up to a random group of women and have them fawning over you within seconds is a strong indication of social grace and intelligence. And when you've completed this book, it's an ability you will possess.

Recognising the Importance of Fashion

In addition to your actual social skills, there is another factor that can be used – and that women in particular *do* use – to gauge your level of social intelligence, and that is your fashion sense. Since the beginning of time fashion has been used to communicate status, and more recently it's become a secret language of coolness. Having good fashion sense communicates that you are socially in tune with what's happening. You know what's cool; you know what's not.

If you think back to school and the kids who were made fun of, there's a good chance that they were dressed in a particularly uncool way. I know this from experience.

On the other hand, if you think about the cool kids, they all probably dressed in clothing similar to each other's. And no matter what that style was, it communicated, 'Hey, I get it; I'm socially accepted.'

Now, when it comes to getting *your* fashion together for the purpose of signalling attractiveness to women, here are my thoughts:

First, be brutally honest with yourself. Most men think that they dress 'just fine'. However, if women aren't complimenting you on how much they like your style, there's a very strong possibility it's *not* fine.

If this sounds like you, it's completely understandable. Outside the fashion industry magazines, there's almost no good material out there for regular guys who want to dress well. I know, because I used to be one of the worst fashion offenders possible. I used to wear sports clothes, baggy jeans and clothing that never got complimented. I dressed for myself, not for women. I was comfortable, sure, but my wardrobe was an absolute mess. Once I decided to ditch my cheap trainers for stylish shoes and traded in my Airwalk hoodie for a suede jacket, I finally started getting compliments and positive attention from women.

After personally transforming my own style and spending hundreds of hours studying the art of coolness when it comes to fashion, along with helping thousands of students trade in their loose-fitting T-shirts for shirts, I developed the following concise list of rules for helping you with your fashion choices:

How to Dress for Success

✓ *Don't dress generically.* If your clothes are so plain that they can't be commented on by a woman, even one trying hard to find something nice to say, then you're generic. If you're wearing drab colours with standard cuts and are generally blending into the background, you're not making the most of your personal style. Look around at other men and see how much you can notice about their sense of style. If their jeans have details and funky touches, those are better than standard Levis. If the jumper or T-shirt has a tailored cut, a slogan, cool detailing, funky colours or a graphic, it's something outside of the generic (i.e. boring) and reflects your personality in a much better way.

✓ *Spend money on the right things.* An expensive shirt or pair of jeans is wasted if your shoes are ugly. Spend a lot of money on a couple of good pairs of shoes (one black, one brown). You can mix cheap (but well-fitting) jeans and shirts with great shoes and you'll look like you're wearing an expensive outfit. After nice shoes, the jacket is the second most important thing (in winter). Next is the shirt or T-shirt, and last are the jeans or trousers. A few great outfits are better than lots of average ones.

✓ *Match clothes correctly.* Blue jeans and brown shoes are better (as in more eye-catching and unique) than blue and black. Don't wear more than three colours in combination. Skinny trousers paired with a baggy shirt are just plain wrong; the fits should all match. More than one bold colour probably means a clash. Sport shoes have no place other than the gym, but brand-new designer trainers are okay.

✓ *Accessorise wisely.* Don't over-accessorise for the sake of it. If you naturally have that surfer style, some beads are great; but if you are a businessman

Peacocking Gone Wrong

Peacocking is the technique of wearing clothes and accessories that attract attention. There's a right way – adopting your own individualistic style – and a wrong way to peacock. Many wannabe ladies' men copy the clothes and accessories of guys who are famously good with women – rock stars who have unique styles, for example. I often see these wannabes around, and they look uncomfortable and forced – like they're wearing something because they *think* they should wear it. It doesn't suit them; it's not a style that represents their character. These guys will get attention, yes; but subconsciously a woman will find their appearance strange. They look weird and stand out in a bad way. If you must peacock, wear things that you like to wear because you think they work for *your* personality.

it'll make you look a little strange. Stick to an interesting watch and a nice leather belt. If at all possible, leave your earrings and nose rings at home.

✓ *Get the best haircut you can afford.* If you're not getting comments on your haircut, you could possibly do better. Go to an expensive salon for a free consultation, find out what would be the best cut for your face shape and hair type, and then get the actual cut done in a cheaper place. And by all means keep it maintained. My 'designer haircut' actually saves me money – I only cut it every three months and use no products!

✓ *Be well groomed.* Get the dirt out from under your fingernails. Brush your teeth. Shine your leather shoes. Keep cologne and aftershave to a bare minimum.

✓ *Look like you're successful and comfortable with women.* Wear your clothes in the right way – unbutton your top buttons, roll your sleeves up. Look around and copy sexy styles. Looking like you're successful with women is something you can't do with generic clothes. Think Colin Farrell, Johnny Depp and David Beckham.

Putting It All Together

The concepts I've just explained and the steps that I've just outlined are the ones that I personally used to change the way I think, feel and behave – both in everyday life and around women. I'm confident that if you follow in my footsteps, you will see very similar results.

At first, taking on new mannerisms and behaviour patterns might seem a bit awkward and clunky. I urge you to keep at it; keep your focus on constantly improving, one day at a time. Eventually, you will look in the mirror one day and you will be blown away by the person you've become. Do your affirmations, build positive emotional patterns and states, work on your body language, practice being assertive and charismatic, and upgrade your fashion. Don't focus on perfection. Just focus on progress.

Keep at it, and I promise you will be pleasantly surprised by the person you become, and of course by the new ways in which women start looking at you and treating you.

3.The Seduction

Now that you know the keys to becoming an attractive male, it's time to master the art of seduction, acquiring the ability to go out any night and take a beautiful woman home, if you so choose.

In this section, I offer you the method I have developed – and use to this day – to meet, attract and sleep with beautiful women.

We begin, in this chapter, by establishing an overarching framework for your interactions – a 'map', if you will – that you can follow from the moment you meet a woman, until the moment you are kissing her goodbye the next morning. Then we will dive into the specifics of each step – the exact methods, techniques and strategies you will be employing to successfully seduce the women you choose.

This is the material that separates the guys who get 'lucky' from the guys who get laid. Study this section carefully – read through each chapter more than once – and then be prepared to take action. There is no limit to what you can achieve, once you do.

The Characters of Seduction

When I first began learning the pickup game, I was literally drowning in information – and misinformation – about being good with women.

One guru would say women want a man who can't be controlled. Another would say women want an emotionally deep man that they can connect with.

One purported expert would say the key is to be the super-social frat-boy kind of guy, while another would say the key is to be a modern-day Don Juan – a smooth, seductive male who cuts through the clutter and romances a girl with poems, roses and fine wine.

The problem for me was that each of these archetypes, when I heard them described, made complete sense. I'd actually *seen* examples of them in the real world – and I'd seen guys like these have massive amounts of success. But as soon as I'd become convinced that one particular way was the *right way,* I'd come upon a different style of seduction, also compelling, that seemed to completely contradict the one that came before.

Overloaded with information and conflicting models of how seduction worked, I hit the 'field' to test them all out on women so as to discover which approach to the game *actually* worked.

And the result wasn't pretty.

Have you ever seen a five-year-old display artistic genius by mixing every colour of the rainbow together and creating a putrid shade of brown?

Well, that's what my game looked like!

One moment I'd be deeply engaged in a discussion about my life story, and the next moment I'd be acting like an arrogant movie star.

Women would just look at me, perplexed that I was changing 'character' so abruptly. Then inevitably they'd kindly (or not so kindly) remove themselves from conversation with me. It really was amazing how many women *suddenly* had to use the bathroom as soon as I got past the five-minute mark with them in a club.

After repeatedly failing, I came to a realisation: there was no *single* correct character to play in a seduction; no one universally applicable seduction persona that works every time.

Instead, I realised, different types of game – different ways of behaving during a seduction – were required at different times during the same interaction.

The way you behave at the start of the seduction is different from the way you behave twenty minutes in. The way you behave twenty minutes in is different from the way you behave when the club is closing down and you're ready to take the girl home.

When I came to this realisation, I began experimenting with different sequences of seduction – acting one way first and then a different way after I'd settled into an interaction. Smoothly transitioning from one character to the next in a way that was consistent moved my interactions forward, and made sense given the context.

After weeks of trial and error I hit upon the perfect model, one I called 'the three characters of seduction'. And when I started using it, wow – my game took off and I never looked back.

Now I'd like to give the model to you.

There are three 'characters', or personas, that the successful man takes on during a seduction. Each of them serves a different purpose. None of them involves 'acting' – it's just a different way of behaving. We all have the capacity to behave in a wide variety of ways, after all. What the three characters model helps you do is structure your behaviour so that you're always acting in a way that maximises your success with women and moves you forward, from the first moment you see a woman you admire to the time you go home with her.

You begin with 'Mr Sociable' upon the initial approach. After you've 'got in' with the girl, you transition to a character I call 'Mr Comfort'; finally, you transition to 'Mr Seducer' when the time is right for you to start leading things towards the bedroom.

The Three Characters in Action

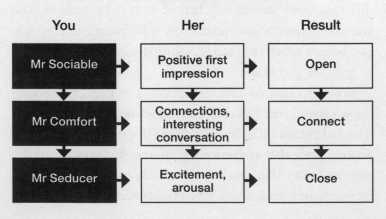

What follows is a description of each of the personas, along with the behavioural characteristics that define them, and famous movie characters you can use as models.

Mr Sociable

This is the guy who makes a great first impression; very animated, he has a high energy level and makes people feel comfortable. He's able to win over any group, make them laugh and generally brighten up their evening. Everyone is glad this person is around because there are no awkward silences; he keeps the conversation going.

Someone who is naturally Mr Comfort and starts an interaction in that role tends to think too much about what he says; he thinks he's being considerate, but the result is off-putting. People relax a lot more when the person they're with is relaxed himself. Mr Sociable personifies this relaxed attitude because he is very natural and says what comes to mind. Because he is comfortable, people relax around him.

On the other hand, although he's very good for the first few minutes, he might find it hard to connect with an individual, or to seduce her, simply because he is *too* high-energy. After a while, women will become tired of talking to him, because he can't be serious or deep. We've all been in situations with someone who constantly cracks jokes; it's good for a few minutes but quickly becomes tiresome. Use this character for only the first few minutes – until you're in a comfortable two-way conversation and you sense that the woman wants you to stick around.

Extroverts will find it easy to step into this role, whereas introverts will find it harder. I knew for a long time that I

needed to be more sociable, outgoing, funny and interesting – but how do you do that?

The Skills of Mr Sociable

✓ Be engaging. As long as people are looking at you
   and listening, they aren't going anywhere and
   you'll be able to get past the first minutes and into
   a conversation. To hold people's attention, you
   can use a few nonverbal techniques. First, hold eye
   contact. If it's one girl, keep a good amount
   of eye contact; if it's a group, spread the eye
   contact around, directing it especially to any
   person who seems to be losing interest. Second,
   use gestures. When you gesture, it catches the eye
   and is a great way to keep attention focused on
   you. Third, be expressive. If you have a poker face,
   people won't feel called to look at you. Fourth,
   vary the tone of your voice, using pauses and
   different pacing. Trying to remove 'ums' and 'ers'
   from your speech will really help your results as
   well.

✓ Be positive. Nobody likes a downer. Although we
   can often connect with people by talking about
   negative stuff, people would much prefer to be
   surrounded by those who make them feel good.
   Always look for the positive, and if someone starts
   a negative conversational thread, try to switch it
   as soon as possible. I'm not talking about being
   in la-la land; you can be realistic, but if you have
   the choice of talking about something negative or
   positive, accentuate the positive.

✓ Enjoy yourself. Smile. Take pleasure in the music, the company, the venue, the drinks, the food. We are always drawn towards people who look like they're having fun. Enthusiasm, passion and happiness are contagious. You will make people want to be part of your life if you look like you're enjoying yourself. One man might be a billionaire with the perfect life but look bored and uninterested; another might be average in every external regard but have a real passion for life. Women will want to be with the second man, because he can make them feel good.

✓ Do most of the talking. Ask few questions. Keep the conversation light and situational.

To further develop these character traits on your own, here are some additional active steps and exercises:

✓ Do something that involves public speaking and being the centre of attention – take a stand-up comedy or acting class, or teach a course as I did, when I spent six weeks in Seville teaching English as a second language.

Examples of Mr Sociable

Owen Wilson and Vince Vaughn as John and Jeremy in *Wedding Crashers*

Ryan Reynolds as Van in *Van Wilder*

✓   Try this acting exercise with a friend: one-word
    improv. The way it works is that you make up
    a story together, one word at a time: you say
    a word ('I') and then your friend says a word
    ('will'), and you continue like this until you've
    got a narrative. (Go. And. See. My. Friends. At.
    The. Beach. And. Build. A. Sandcastle. Then ...)
    When you come to a full stop, you use words like
    'next', 'afterwards' and 'then' to carry it on. If
    you manage to increase the speed as you get good
    at this, the skill should translate directly into
    natural conversation.

Mr Comfort

After you've integrated into a group or made initial contact
with a woman, you can bring out Mr Comfort. When you
first approach strangers, they're usually in a wait-and-see
mode. It might happen quickly, or might take a while,
but soon they will open up to you and commit to the
interaction. How do you know when this has happened?
Nonverbally: they will stop looking at each other, or
around the room, and focus on you and what you're saying.
Verbally: they will start to commit more to the conversation, giving longer answers and asking you questions.

While Mr Comfort isn't as outgoing as Mr Sociable,
he's no slouch in the interaction department. Mr Comfort
is interested and interesting. He listens about 50 per cent
of the time, doesn't talk too much about himself and tries
to understand women, find common interests and build
rapport. He should stick around until you've established a
palpable connection with a girl, at which point he should

start to bring in some elements of the next character, Mr Seducer. Usually, Mr Comfort can't start conversations very well and isn't very seductive, so it's awkward when he goes in for a kiss.

Most introverts will be at home in this mode. The problem is getting stuck in it! Ninety per cent of the time, when guys tell me they've been put into the 'friend zone' by a woman, it's due to being Mr Comfort for too long. Giving off no sexual vibe, no matter how good you are conversationally, means you're of no more use to her than her girlfriends or gay best friend!

The Skills of Mr Comfort

- ✓ Listen actively. When others are speaking, don't just stand there waiting to jump in. Look them in the eye, nod your head and encourage them to continue.

- ✓ Imagine that you've known the person you're speaking to for your entire life. Project the feeling of fondness you have for your oldest and best of friends and watch as this new acquaintance reciprocates.

Examples of Mr Comfort

David Schwimmer as Ross in the TV show *Friends*

Martin Freeman as Tim in the TV show *The Office*

Jason Segel as Peter in *Forgetting Sarah Marshall*

✓ Humanise yourself – paint a picture of who you are, where you're from (your history) and what you're all about. Don't brag; simply open up and allow your conversational partner to see you for who you are. Don't be afraid to poke fun at yourself and talk about the time you embarrassed yourself at your birthday party when you were eight years old. Imperfection is lovable.

Mr Seducer

The Seducer is the man who is unapologetic about his sexual intention towards a woman. While he doesn't come out and overtly say, 'Hey, I want to sleep with you!', he does give signals to the woman that he's very interested, in a smooth, almost calculated way. Be it the way he looks at the woman, the way he holds her hand or the way he uses his voice, Mr Seducer is the guy who can get the girl into bed.

The Mr Seducer character doesn't just pop out of left field when you need him. Instead, he emerges gradually, the more you find out about a woman. This way, your attraction to her is justified and, in her eyes, is not based on looks alone.

The Skills of Mr Seducer

✓ Don't be afraid to reveal your desire. Look the woman in the eyes in a way that communicates, 'I want you tonight.'

✓ Slow down the rate at which you speak.

Examples of Mr Seducer

Ryan Phillippe as Sebastian in *Cruel Intentions*

Johnny Depp as John in *Don Juan DeMarco*

Brad Pitt as Joe in *Meet Joe Black*

✓ As you begin to speak more slowly, add pauses …
  in the way … you speak … while still holding solid
  eye contact. Pauses in the middle … of sentences
  are … especially powerful.

✓ Introduce touching and physicality with more
  frequency and intimacy.

✓ Reduce movement and make sure any body
  movement, gestures and touches fit with the slow,
  smooth, seductive rhythm.

These three characters provide the general framework
for what to do when you interact with a woman. It's a
map, if you will. What we'll do in the chapters that follow
is zoom down to 'street level' and look at the nitty-gritty
of how you actually navigate through the seduction each
step of the way. We'll learn how to master the skills of each
character, and how to tie them all together, step-by-step,
so that when you go out and meet women, success is practically guaranteed.

4. The Approach

It all begins with the approach – the moment you lay eyes on a woman you want and make your first steps towards her. Most guys fear the approach. They see it as a scary situation, where the odds of success are low and the chances of brutal rejection are all too high. And you know what? This is completely justified for guys who have no game plan, no technique and no strategy for smoothly and confidently getting in the door. After you've read the pages that follow, though, you will. And for you, the approach will no longer be a numbers game.

Opening Cold vs Opening Warm

A cold approach is when you initiate a conversation with a girl and are unsure of the response you'll get. She hasn't shown prior interest in you and may not even have noticed you. A warm approach is one where you think the response will be at least somewhat positive because you've already made eye contact or received some sign of interest, like a smile, a wink or a quick glance before looking away.

Obviously, if all of our approaches could be warm approaches, the results would be a lot more successful and less stressful. But there are ways of having a successful approach, no matter what.

Standing Out in a Positive Way

Being Mr Sociable and talking to people *other than* the hottest women will disarm that super-hot girl you're really after. She'll see you having fun with people, and by the time you get near her she'll be a lot more open and receptive to your advances. This is easier than trying to stand out in a club by being super-cool and aloof, since many other guys are trying to do the same thing.

This approach has the added benefit of loosening you up and giving you a chance to practise your sociability skills.

Forcing Her Interest

Most guys deal with eye contact from a girl in one of three ways. Is one of these *your* response of choice?

- ✓ Nervously look away.
- ✓ Hold eye contact until she looks away.
- ✓ Force a smile.

These are all pretty bad, unfortunately. Even the second one, which may strike you as the 'right' answer since I've been urging good eye contact, isn't effective because – barring any other response on your part – the held contact will feel forced to her and she'll look away out of pure discomfort.

It's a conundrum, to be sure. And it may be a deal-breaker if you don't know how to handle it. If you're wondering why a girl is looking at you, you may use the uncertainty as an excuse not to approach. Maybe she was looking at someone else; maybe you have a spot on your nose; maybe she was just daydreaming. In 90 per cent of cases, she *is* looking at you and would welcome your approach, but there's always the other 10 per cent, and that's enough to discourage most guys from approaching.

How many missed opportunities have you suffered over the years? Potential girlfriends, girls that would have loved to sleep with you and maybe even that special 'one'. I can make sure you never miss an opportunity like that ever again.

Here's what to do: force her interest!

When you've made eye contact with the girl, provoke a response from her by doing something along these lines: pointing at her; waving; raising your glass; making a funny face; poking your tongue out. If you use this technique, you will be in very good company. Over the years, I've met many great naturals as well as professional seduction coaches who, independent of each other, have come up with this technique. They all do it slightly differently, but the idea is the same. Cardenas, one of the most alpha naturals I've ever met, who is the typical gym buff with big muscles, pokes his tongue out. It's a great contrast to his tough-guy look. Rob, who is my age but had slept with seven hundred women by the time I'd slept with only seven, hides his face behind his hands and does a childish peek-a-boo. It sounds stupid, but the results speak for themselves. Steve, the best seducer I've ever seen, draws an imaginary pistol and shoots his intended 'target' with it while smiling playfully. Personally, I do my trademark 'point'. I guess it looks like something Joey from *Friends* would do. To see a video of how I force an indication of interest (IOI), go to www.puatraining.com/forceioi.

The point of all these actions is that they're so bold that the girl is compelled to respond. The number of responses she can give is limited. She can:

✓ Mirror your action.

✓ Smile.

✓ Smile and look away, embarrassed.

✓ Look away in disgust.

✓ Raise an eyebrow as if to say, 'What are you doing?'

If you get a positive reaction, you can immediately approach without needing to think of anything clever to say. If you get a negative reaction, you probably won't get a good one if you go on and attempt to 'open'. The secret to success is that your trademark will become a reflex action. It's as if you'd studied kung fu for twenty years, so you swing into action without thinking twice when someone attacks you.

Believe me, it takes a lot more balls to approach a beautiful woman cold than to force her interest. So start practicing your own signature moves, or be my guest and steal my trademark point. By the way, to show just how important this is, keep this in mind: with more than 80 per cent of the women I've talked to in the past three years, the initial conversation has been as a result of this technique!

Approaching After an Indication of Interest

If she gave you a sign of interest, it's doubtful that she's not attracted, so go for it! I usually use, 'Hey, how's it going?' Longer or indirect openers (like asking for an opinion about this or that) will kill tension. Just be bold, be direct, and assume that she's attracted to you.

Using Body Language to Maximise the Cold Approach

There are two ways to make a cold approach. One is the cold walk-up, where you directly approach a girl and engage her. The second is a more casual, seemingly spontaneous way to open: the girl is a step or two away, and you casually turn around, or move closer, and open. In both instances, there are steps you can take to create a favourable first impression.

What you 'say' with your body can either advance your cause or doom you to failure. Let's look first at some common body language faux pas.

Weak Body Language

Most men walk up to a girl they're interested in and get right in her face. Do this to someone you *know* and it's bad enough. Ask someone to do this to you to see how it feels. It creates a reflex response of wanting to step back

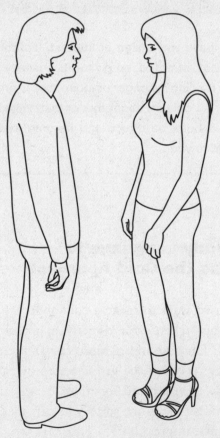

This example is bad in so many ways. It's very locked in; the stance is statuesque; the head is the furthest part forward of the body. A woman will feel very uncomfortable if this is your body language on a cold approach. If this is how you're standing when you first open your mouth, then what you say will have to be pretty incredible to make a favourable impression!

So what does this communicate? It's not scary or creepy, but it's very weak. Look how an attractive man can be made to look very unattractive with awful body language. Hands in pockets, an approval-seeking tilt of the head and an unsure posture all communicate weakness. This is not the pose of a comfortable, confident man.

and put your hands up to create distance. This puts a lot of pressure on an interaction before it has even begun. Unless the girl is obviously interested in you, it's a bad move. This type of face-to-face interaction also feels like it could go on forever because it's so awkward. Both people look locked in, and the only way for the interaction to end is if someone turns one hundred and eighty degrees. In the event of a flat-out rejection, everyone around you has seen what happened, so you're putting even more pressure on yourself.

Once you understand body language and can read women's reactions, you'll see how bad at this most men are. This is the kind of knowledge that will boost confidence, because you know that you understand how to do things better than most other men.

Strong Body Language

When you're opening, your feet should be pointing away from the girl; only your face should be pointing towards her. By adopting this posture, you can comfortably get close enough to touch, but the interaction isn't as locked in and you aren't invading her personal space.

To 'eject' – to remove yourself from the interaction – you'd just have to turn your head and not face her anymore. I think most people respond well to being 'opened' this way, because they've probably already had many short, innocent interactions similar to this prior to your making your move.

The low-pressure way to open is with the feet pointing away from the girl and only the face pointing towards her. Because this looks impermanent, it's very comfortable for the girl. It also seems more spontaneous.

Here we have a better posture; it's open and more confident. There's eye contact, yes; but any potential threat is lessened by the head being in line with the body and by the use of gestures. One foot is pointing away, which makes the stance feel less locked in and more casual.

Using Body Language with a Seated Group

When you approach a seated group, you want to quickly get down to the same level as the girl you're interested in, because it's very difficult to open – much less close – when you're standing over someone.

You probably haven't had this happen since school, but someone standing over you will put you on guard immediately. If you approach a girl from a standing position, sit down within ten seconds. You can use a time constraint – 'I need to go soon, but just wanted to ask you ...' – to avoid making her feel uncomfortable at sitting with someone she has just met.

If there are no spare chairs, or if you need to ask her to move to make space for you, you should start off in a position like this so that you're on her level. But don't stay like this for too long or it will become weird. Quickly ask her to move over; alternatively, move yourself to sit on the arm of the chair or even share her chair with her.

On the other hand, if when she catches your eye she stands up, the aforementioned recommendations for body language immediately apply.

These examples will help you perfect the indirect approach. Direct game (showing interest right away) obviously requires that you put more pressure on an interaction earlier on, so making the girl feel comfortable and minimising your chances of getting rejected aren't so much of an issue. Direct body language is all about presenting a sexual vibe, touching quickly and escalating sexually.

The Two Schools of Seduction

There are two very distinct schools of seduction, direct or indirect, and most methods fall into one of them. The system presented in this book takes both into account, and I suggest that you use them both, depending on the circumstances.

Direct Game

Direct game involves approaching, immediately conveying interest, then rapidly intensifying the interaction with words and kino-escalation (a.k.a. increasingly sexual touches – a touch on the arm, then the small of back; then holding hands, stroking through her hair, kissing, etc.). An example of direct game is to approach a girl, tell her you think she's beautiful, then take her by the hands and quickly go for the kiss. You're basically approaching in seduction mode (that is, as Mr Seduction – one of the three characters of seduction introduced in the previous chapter). The benefit of a direct approach is its efficiency. It allows you to quickly test a girl's interest. Who wants to wait hours to kiss if they don't have to? Who wants to chat for an hour before finding out the girl is unavailable?

The drawbacks of direct game are:

✓ It requires a high degree of personal and sexual confidence in order to be successful.

✓ It generates more approach anxiety by putting you on the line and adding pressure to the interaction.

✓ You may be rejected from a group that would have been receptive to a slower, more subtle approach.

✓ Women generally need more time to warm up to a potential partner than guys do, and they consider the first impression to be less important than men do.

Indirect Game

Indirect game is basically coming in under the radar, getting the girl comfortable with you, and slowly introducing a sexual vibe. The benefits of an indirect approach are:

✓ It reduces approach anxiety by minimising the chance of getting rejected.

✓ It's easier when dealing with a group, which may take some time to 'infiltrate'.

✓ It involves more and longer interactions, which allow you to get comfortable talking to women and to practise your conversational skills.

The drawbacks of an indirect approach are:

✓ Sometimes she wants you and you lose her because she doesn't think you're interested.

✓ You can waste time on a girl you have no chance with (she'll never find you attractive, she's engaged, she's a lesbian), and you don't find out until late in the interaction because she thinks you're just being friendly.

I suggest you use direct game when you're getting a clear sign of interest. If you're not quite sure, take the indirect route. I also suggest that your approaches remain indirect until you have a lot of experience in reading situations and have overcome approach anxiety. If I have a client who has a huge fear of talking to women, I'll ensure that his first few approaches are spent doing things like asking for directions – which is as indirect as you can get.

Maximising Interactions

In a club or bar environment, if you limit yourself to cold approaches you're making things difficult for yourself. There are plenty of opportunities around you at all times to help create easier interactions.

Picking Up on Inadvertent Cues

One of the simplest and least obtrusive things you can do is simply take advantage of cues and lead-ins that women give you inadvertently. Consider these options:

- ✓ A women stepping on your foot: 'Hey, watch it punk!' *(Square up to her with a smirk.)* 'Let's take this outside; let me see what you've got!' *(Flex your upper arm and point for her to do likewise – then feel her muscle.)*

- ✓ A women squeezing past with drinks: 'Cheers!'

- ✓ A women pushing past rudely: 'No, my dear, do it like this.' *(Demonstrate the polite way to move past.)* 'Excuse me, sir.'

All of the above will allow you to get into interactions without the pressure and effort of a cold approach.

Working the Room

One of the best ways to warm up cold approaches is to do a little groundwork by working the room. In the context of pickup this involves talking to all the groups you're interested in, as well as some others in the room, all the time staying very indirect. At the end of a short interaction, the key is to act as if you're about to leave that particular group and then, as if an afterthought, get the name of any girl who's caught your interest. What you'll be able to do in a short amount of time is:

✓ Meet (and learn the names of) all the girls you are attracted to.

✓ Create a positive, safe, nonthreatening impression in their heads – that you're not so desperate that you have to hang around them until they tell you to go away.

✓ Establish yourself as Mr Sociable. After you've done this, you'll be able to reopen any of these groups at any time during the night. You'll also notice a big increase in interest from girls that you've already opened. Getting the first name (and remembering it!) is the key factor. I found out by chance that reopening with the name is much more effective, as the girl will actually treat you like someone she's known for a long time.

This technique is best used in smaller places, early on in the evening. That way, as the night progresses and people open up, your options will continue to increase. Plus you won't have the problem of opening when it gets louder and more crowded ... and more competitive.

I used to work the room at a small club in London that I went to regularly. One time I arranged to meet a friend there, but picked up a girl on the way and brought her with me. Now I was in the difficult position of being with a girl I wanted to spend time with, but also having to leave my poor friend on his own. To resolve the dilemma, I asked her to wait for a minute, and I went with my friend around the whole club, said 'Hi' to everyone, took some names, chatted for thirty seconds, made sure my buddy met them all, and then went on to the next group. I did this to everyone in the club, and on the way back literally every girl in the place was staring at me. I'd warmed up the entire club, and my friend could easily reopen any of the girls there. He used my female pal and me as a base in the club, coming back between

Assignment No.2

Go to a bar, buy a drink, and go around 'cheers-ing' everyone. You will find that people will always 'cheers' you back, and afterward you will get a lot of attention from girls wondering why you didn't try to pick them up. It's an easy way to work the room because it removes the need to think of anything to say!

interactions, but was easily able to get a lot of numbers because he already had huge social proof as a fun-loving, sociable guy, who seemed to know everyone. If he forgot a name, he could come back and ask me because I'd memorised them all.

Overcoming Transition and Approach Anxiety

Most men feel a little or even a lot of anxiety as they attempt to meet and get to know women. Transition anxiety and approach anxiety are two of the most common types.

Transition Anxiety

When doing something outside your comfort zone, you'll naturally find it scary. Transition anxiety is best described as the feeling you get in your stomach at any time like this. Whether it's the thought of riding a scary roller coaster, jumping out of a plane to skydive, signing up for a course, meeting new people at a party, taking a test, speaking in public or approaching a woman – what all these things share in common is that they may give us butterflies in our stomach, to varying degrees.

This feeling holds us back; it doesn't serve us well. Anything that we haven't done before – that puts us in an uncertain situation we don't feel equipped for – causes at least some transition anxiety. That would be fine if the feeling were saving us from getting eaten by a lion or doing something truly hazardous, but generally it's only stopping us from improving, learning and changing.

Each one of us has a comfort zone within which we can safely stay inside – a daily routine or people we know. However, remaining in this comfort zone makes it hard to make big changes or improvements to your life. If you look back and remember all the times you've felt transition anxiety and taken action anyway, you'll see that each time it has impacted your life in a positive way. Whether it was moving to a new area, changing jobs or taking a class, these were likely things that benefited you greatly.

A man who decides to get a handle on his life will feel transition anxiety before he clicks the sign-up button on our website. Lots of others will feel that anxiety and simply never click the button. It's a fact!

So what about those crazy people who always try new things and never seem to feel uncomfortable? If anything, they appear to welcome uncertain new situations.

Let me assure you: it's not just appearances. They really have changed that feeling in their stomach from something that holds them back to something that kicks them into action. This is what I've done. I used to be a complete scaredy-cat when it came to almost anything that involved leaving my house! Now anytime I get that feeling, I know that I should take action and that, by the end of it, I'll be a better person. As a result, fewer and fewer things intimidate me; in fact, I feel like I can handle almost anything. Embrace transition anxiety and you'll be thanking me later. That step will affect every area of your life positively and will make you a better person.

Approach Anxiety

Approaching a woman you're attracted to is one of the scariest things a guy can do. You know it doesn't make sense to be as afraid to initiate an interaction as you would be to fight someone who's trying to rob you. After all, in one situation, the worst that can happen is that she says no; in the second, the worst that can happen is serious physical injury. Yet over 95 per cent of the people I work with have some degree of approach anxiety. Conquering it isn't something that neurolinguistic programming or affirmations can provide a quick fix for. There is no easy way to get over it. However, I can tell you the most painless way possible: in my experience, thirty approaches will be enough to free you of crippling approach anxiety. You might still have some with each encounter, but you'll be opening enough groups to get along.

First, let's take away some of the fear (or 'outcome dependency'). As long as you have a lot of approach anxiety, work on that first, before refining your overall technique. In your first approaches, don't 'open to close'; just open and eject – in other words: practise opening. Just go up and ask, 'What's the time?' Thanking her and leaving is a lot easier than approaching with the intention of getting her back to your place.

The next thing you can do is use indirect openers. These minimise the chance of rejection and allow you to practise opening without caring whether the girl you're chatting up is attracted or has a boyfriend.

Finally, it helps not to be too fussy. Practise opening and extending the interaction, but do it with *any* group. Don't try to conquer your fear or practise pickup skills only with women you find super hot. That would take too long. You need to be out there practicing, opening twenty groups a day. You have to be focused on practicing, not on closing.

When I first started going out to work on my skills, I forced myself to do as many approaches a night as possible. I would do as many as twenty in a few hours. It gave me a buzz to be talking to so many attractive women who I'd never met before. I must have talked to more women in just a few weeks than I'd done in my entire life up to that point! I love female energy and being in the company of pretty women, so I was happy just to have these short interactions.

Doing lots of approaches at first not only helps you desensitise yourself and remove approach anxiety, but it also helps you get out of your own head and get focused on the other person. When you're thinking a lot about your own body language, your voice, what you're saying, what you're going to do next, you can't focus enough on the other person to read signals and give her what she wants.

During my first thirty or so approaches after deciding to work on my skills with women, I'd be talking to a girl, but most of my attention would be focused on what to say next, how my body language was, whether my voice was loud enough, whether my sweaty palms would turn her off and I'd miss all the little signals that she was giving me.

I remember approaching two girls in a coffee shop early on in my training. I saw that they had a London Underground Tube map and, without thinking much, I approached and asked if I could look at it to see how to get to Earl's Court. Since they seemed friendly enough in passing over the map, I asked them where they were from. They were Czech, they said, and studying English in London. I was laughing nervously and blushing as we talked, but I also felt a bit euphoric – I was getting a positive reaction! I did something I'd never done before: I talked for what seemed like minutes (but was probably not more than twenty seconds) about how I'd gone to Seville and got a TEFL qualification.

This was the first time I'd had serious attention from a couple of girls focused on me for more than a few seconds. It was a real breakthrough, *because I forged ahead*. Prior to this I'd just asked questions to avoid having the attention focused on me.

I still messed up, though. When I asked what they were doing later, they said they had to meet a friend soon. Swallowing my disappointment, I said, 'Oh, okay. Bye then.' I took what they said in the worst possible way, assuming that they were trying to hint that they weren't interested, and sat back down. As they were leaving, they hung around expectantly, but I didn't have the courage to reopen and ask for their number. A common mistake guys make is hitting the self-destruct button, as I did on that occasion: they take the tiniest negative thing as an excuse to run away. Practice helps curb that urge to run.

'Assignments' can also get you over approach anxiety. Give yourself assignments each time you go out. Test openers or see how many groups you can engage, for example. Go out with a friend and push each other into action. Find out what your motivation is and when you perform well. I perform well under pressure, so it helps me to tell the guys I'll open any group they want me to. Other people might want to dare or bet each other. Try some different things and find out what will make your approach happen. Some guys do better with a wingman, so experiment there too. (See chapter 10 for tips on wingmen.)

Framing an Uncomfortable Situation

Some situations just feel uncomfortable. Approaching a girl you've really got the hots for, and knowing you'll be crushed if she rejects you because you haven't had sex in six months, is destined to be uncomfortable. Going to a club on your own probably will be too. However, most of the discomfort from these situations has to do with your mental frame. By framing a situation differently, you can actually put yourself at ease.

I frequently do this for self-conscious people in my one-on-one trainings: I get them to stand for one minute in a very busy street and look straight ahead – no fidgeting, no shifting around, no looking down. They inevitably feel uncomfortable, as if everyone is looking at them. I then tell them to repeat the exercise, imagining that a friend of theirs is going to appear in the distance around the corner and that they're waiting to go have coffee with him. They do it again and it's usually completely comfortable for them.

Similarly, being alone in a club can be framed so that you're completely comfortable – you're waiting for a friend. You were meant to meet at the entrance, but he texted to say he's running late and will be there in an hour. Now you can be more comfortable in the club on your own, though nothing has really changed. It's like method acting.

You can also apply this to approaching women. Instead of having a pickup frame in your head, try framing the situation as, 'I'm a fun, sociable guy. I'm going to talk to lots of people, and if I happen to have a good interaction with a girl I find attractive, closing will be natural.' This is a much healthier frame and also removes a lot of the approach anxiety, outcome dependency and neediness. You should try to reframe any situation in which you feel uncomfortable.

Additional Resource

If you want to dive *deep* into doing belief change work and really 'reboot' your psychology, we have a programme available called 'Inner Game: Installed'. Guys absolutely rave about the programme and you can find more about it by going to the following URL: www.puatraining.com/inner gameinstalled/.

5. The Opener

You've made the approach. Now it's time to open. The opener is quite simply the first words that come out of your mouth. Most guys leave this to chance; they rely on luck or hope. Not us, though. In this chapter you will learn what to say to women upon the

The First Minute

The first minute of a pickup is the most important. In this time, you will have identified a girl, got into state, overcome any approach anxiety, positioned yourself, opened and hopefully achieved a 'hook point'. Normally, by the end of the first minute you know how receptive your girl is and whether or not you have a realistic chance of success.

approach and then what to say just afterwards to transition smoothly into an interaction that feels natural and unforced.

The Pre-Opener: Just Say 'Hey'

Believe it or not, all openers should start with 'Hey.' This pre-opener is an important element, and because it's counterintuitive – I mean, you expect that first word to be *meaningful*, right? – it needs to be explained.

Think about it: if you deliver an opener to a woman or a group, most of the time you'll be interrupting something. They will likely be in conversation already, or at least thinking about something with a conversation going on inside their head. When you start talking, you're breaking that state, and their response will be, 'What?' In fact, they'll say, 'What?', even if they heard what you said. Think about how you do this in your own life; be aware of your interaction next time you join a group.

I only learned this properly when I started as a trainer and watched students open without first saying, 'Hey.' The girls would say, 'What?' and the interaction always seemed to go badly after that. It got the guys off on the wrong foot from the beginning.

The 'Hey' is followed by a pause, to ensure that you have the attention of the group *before* you deliver your actual opener. It's 'Hey!' *(Pause as group looks at you.)* 'Do you guys …' Actually, you've got a little leeway here: the pre-opener can be anything that gets the attention of the group: 'Hey!' or 'Oi!' or 'Howdy!' or even something nonverbal, like a raised hand, a funny or inquisitive facial

Transitioning from a Good Opener

Friends are always asking me what are the best openers, but what they don't realise is that the transition is actually more important than the opener. The most important thing is what you follow the opener with. That's why, until you can freestyle on your own, you need to know your opener and also the transition before you start an interaction.

If you open with, 'Hey, should I dye my hair blond?' and the girl says, 'Yes,' and you say, 'Okay, thanks – bye,' you haven't accomplished anything. You need to know what you'll follow it up with. So you can use that opener and then your transition might be, 'Cool, because my hairdresser tells me every time I go there that I'd look great with blond hair. He's a great hairdresser and knows his stuff, but he's gay, so I really wasn't sure on this one. Actually, I say he's gay because I just think he is, but on the other hand he tries to talk about women. He just *looks* gay. Do you think you can tell when a man is gay?' If you go in with that much prepared, you have enough to get to the hook point in the majority of cases. If you have *just* the opener ready, you'll be putting a lot more pressure on yourself.

Personally I don't think the opener is that important, and I prove this with students by asking for the lamest opener possible and still showing that I can hook or close.

continued

An example would be, 'My elbow hurts,' which was one given to me by a one-on-one student who thought the opener was key. I went up to a seated pair of girls without knowing what I'd come up with as a transition, and actually used, 'I was testing the theory that you can use anything to start a conversation.' They were initially very negative, but even after this lame opener they opened up after a minute or so; I stayed for fifteen minutes and got one of their numbers.

expression or some other action that makes the girl or group stop what they're doing and look at you.

Elements of a Successful Opener

The opener is the first *real* thing you say during an interaction, once you've taken the stage with your pre-opener. The best openers make your audience laugh, make you look cool and are much more interesting than whatever the girls were discussing before you came along.

There are various types of openers. An indirect opener is one that doesn't immediately convey your interest in her and doesn't put much pressure into the interaction. If you say, 'You're hot and I want you,' that's very direct and puts a lot of pressure on her, but if you say, 'When does it get busy here?' there's no pressure.

Opinion openers, a common form of indirect opener that we'll talk about later, work very well in bars and quiet clubs; time and time again I've seen a guy use them to successfully hook or connect to a group. For now, though, let's look at some basic indirect lines.

Indirect Openers

Here are some indirect openers and how they might be used. Different people feel comfortable saying different kinds of things. You can pick a few from below, modify them to fit you better and, later, make up your own. You don't need hundreds. A couple of solid, tried-and-tested openers are enough.

- **Are you guys talking about me? ... Why not?**

Humour is the approach here. The key is making certain that the first line is deadpan and the second is delivered with a smile. Women are attracted to the unexpected. When they realise that they've fallen into your line, they'll laugh and become interested in you.

- **There's a guy over there who is so perfect for you!**

This opener involves approaching a woman, pointing to a guy you (supposedly) think is 'perfect' for her and trying to take her over to meet him. Invariably she'll refuse and then you can say how she should trust you because you're a great matchmaker. That opener leads nicely into conversation on dating and relationships. Her objection is projected onto the other guy, so you've got less chance of getting rejected yourself. It also provides a false disqualifier, meaning something that hides the fact that you are hitting on her, ultimately making it easier to hook a group.

- **You are so … in my way.**

If you've got a situation where you're walking and a girl you're interested in blocks your path, put your hand up as if to gesture her to stop.

Look at her seriously and deliver the line. The key is the pause; it makes her think you're going to say, 'You are so beautiful' or some other clichéd statement. If you do it right, it guarantees a laugh. I used to use it when I first started, and the girls would laugh but still carry on walking afterwards – so you need to quickly introduce yourself in order to extend the opening.

- **Are you girls sociable/friendly?**

Standard opener – can be delivered with a sceptical face. Be ready for a yes or no answer and have a follow-up ready.

- **Are you girls super-shy or what? I've been here for ten minutes and you haven't offered to buy me a drink or even said 'Hello'.**

This one puts them on the spot slightly and then releases the tension; they'll laugh if it's delivered right.

- **Are you rich chicks?**

This allows the funny follow-up, 'I'm looking for a rich girl who can buy me stuff.' I use this successfully, but, as with all the other one-liners, don't expect it to be a magic bullet. You still need to work a bit more to reach the hook point.

- **Did you invite all these people? I thought it'd just be us.**

This is a semi-direct approach, but the pressure is softened by its humour.

- **I know you probably get no attention from guys whatsoever, so I thought I'd come and make some conversation with you.**

This one should get a laugh. You'll be on the spot after this, though, so have something to follow it up with.

- *(Primp an item of her clothing)* **What's your name?**

This one is good for a girl with a hat or some other kind of striking accessory. You look at her, do a double-take, focus your attention on the item and screw your face up as if something is wrong. Hold out a finger as if to say, 'Wait,' adjust the item, then study her again and make a thumbs-up. Don't let the opener end there, though; otherwise that'll be it. Follow it up with something like this:

> **You:** What's your name?
>
> **Her:** Tanya.
>
> **You:** Tanya, I've just made you 38 per cent more attractive. You owe me!

- **Hey, I'm out meeting people tonight; what's your name?**

Standard, low-risk opener that fits a Mr Sociable frame.

- **Are you undressing me with your eyes?**

If a girl is making eye contact with you, this is a good opener to use. By way of variation, you can accuse girls of stalking you, checking you out, etc.

- **My girlfriend thinks you're hot.**

This line uses fake social proof, a guy with a girlfriend being higher value than a single guy out on the prowl, to make it easier to open. Point to some random hot girl as your 'girlfriend'. Later it can be revealed that she's just a female friend, and you're in fact single – although you're friends with lots of girls.

- **Are you girls making mischief over here?**

This is a funny one, and the delivery is important: suspicion mixed with playfulness works well. You might add that they look shifty, like they're going to steal something.

- **My friend wants to know if you think I'm hot.**

This is a fairly direct opener that offsets the direct question by asking it from a friend's point of view.

- **I know that look. Are you girls male bashing?**

When you see women talking seriously, you can open with this. Chances are they're talking about men, and so will laugh. If not, they'll still probably laugh because they know that they often are male bashing.

- **How's it going? We're out picking up chicks.**

This approach works purely because it's funny. If you deliver the lines right, you'll get a laugh. It's important to make sure they know that you're joking. Otherwise this turns into a *direct* approach.

• **Are you listening to our conversation? ... Then why are you acting so nervous?**

This is a good way to open a group that is standing near you. You can follow up with something like this:

> **You:** So what do you think?
>
> **Her:** About what?
>
> **You:** About what we were talking about.
>
> **Her:** We weren't listening!
>
> **You:** Okay, well, we were talking about whether ...

From here you can segue easily into an opinion opener (again, more on those later).

• **Which of you girls gets hit on the most?**

This is a pretty good opener for two attractive girls who look kind of different to each other.

• **Are you confident enough to accept a sincere compliment? ... Good, so am I – you go first.**

This is a classic, and it will usually make them laugh. However, it can sometimes fall flat after they chuckle, so make sure you have something ready to follow up with.

• **Are you single? So when are you asking me out? Are you nervous?**

This one works very well because it puts the girl on the spot and gets her frustrated. You can then release the pressure by nudging her and laughing or saying, 'Wow, you're really cute when you're mad.' You want to fire the questions in quick succession without giving her much time to think or answer fully.

- **If I didn't have a girlfriend and wasn't gay, you'd so be mine.**

This is a variation on saying you're either gay or have a girlfriend. I think this one is better, though, because most people don't want to mislead a girl into thinking they're gay or have a girlfriend – and saying *both* suggests that neither is true. It's also confusing, of course – but her subconscious will get that you're actually saying, 'Be mine'.

- **Hey, sorry I'm late.**

How the hell do you approach a big group who are waiting in the street or sitting at a table in a bar/club? In this way: talk about how the traffic was terrible; you're Paul's cousin or Bob's nephew – whatever. It's funny. When you get caught out, don't dwell on it. Ask some names and find out what's going on, then proceed as normal.

- **You have very thoughtful eyes. I think you have a lot going on inside here. *(Touch her head.)***

This is a good direct line to use on a girl who looks bored. Most guys go in with, 'You look bored.' That's never going to work, but this variation is a nice direct compliment.

- **Hey, I have a policy of meeting the hottest girl in the club when I go out. My name's Rich. *(Shake hands.)* So, do you know her? *(Point at another hot girl.)***

Remember to deliver the first line deadpan and the second line with a big smile. She'll probably give you a punch on the arm. Don't worry: this means the opener worked and she likes you.

Opinion Openers

Opinion openers, a subcategory of indirect openers, are the easiest way for a newbie to start a conversation in a quiet club or bar. They're good in that they can get a long conversation started pretty easily. A well-crafted opinion opener can guarantee you a few minutes of conversation in which to make a connection.

You've got two delivery options: you can either make it seem spontaneous or 'root' it. A spontaneous opinion opener comes from reacting to something your friend supposedly said and simply asking whoever is nearest – who just happen to be a pair of hot chicks! – what *they* think. Rooting the opener means that you tell them the reason you're asking, so that they know why they're spending their time giving you their advice.

All of the examples below include roots, but remember that you can always go down the spontaneous route if the situation calls for it.

- **How soon is too soon to get engaged?**

Here's how you might deliver this one: 'You look like you can help me with something. My friend is coming in an hour and he needs my advice. He's known his girlfriend for three months and he's going to ask her to marry him tomorrow. He says he wants my advice, but I think he's already made his mind up. I think it's too soon, but if I tell him that he might never talk to me again. On the other hand, if I say it's a good idea and it doesn't work out, I'll feel responsible. So what do you guys think, how soon is too soon to get engaged?'

This is a fantastic opener that leads straight into relationship talk and has a lot of drama built in. It should hook very well.

● **What kind of present should I get for my friend's girlfriend?**

'Hey, I need your advice on something. My best friend had to rush away on business – he's got the biggest business deal of his life going – and he's asked me a massive favour. He's given me a couple of hundred pounds and asked me to get a present for his girlfriend. He's done so much for me over the years, so I said I'd take care of it. I really want to get it right. I've been giving it some thought, but I'm pretty stuck. Do you have any ideas?'

This is a great one for the daytime, in shops and malls, but it can also be used at night. It's very flexible and also very engaging because it hits a great topic – shopping and gifts!

● **How should my friend deal with his jealous girlfriend?**

Picture this conversation:

> **You:** Hey, guys, let me get your opinion on something. I'm trying to give my friend over there advice, but we're just a bunch of guys and don't feel qualified to comment on these matters. Okay, well, my friend has been dating a girl for three months, and she just moved in with him. Now, this is a two-part question. Here's the first part. So, imagine you've been

dating someone for three months and he's still friends with his old girlfriend from university. How do you feel about that?

Girls: That depends. Are they just friends?

You: Yes, they're *just* friends. There's nothing else going on. They talk like once a week at most.

Girls: I think it's fine. / I don't think they should be talking. / Whatever.

You: Okay, now let's say that he has a drawer in his flat. And in that drawer he keeps all of his old photographs and letters. Now, some of those letters happen to be from exes and some of the photographs happen to be with exes.

Girls: Blah, blah, blah – concerned comment – blah, blah, blah – question.

You: It's not like he ever looks at them. They're just there, like old souvenirs and memories of his past.

Girls: I think it's fine. / I think he should destroy them. / Whatever.

- **What do you think of piercings?**

I deliver this one as follows: 'Hey, gals, what do you think of piercings? My ex-girlfriend was a bit of a rock chick, and she always used to say, "You should get a piercing *here*."(*Pinch eyebrow to show where it would go.*) I'm not going out with her anymore, but I'm still kind of considering it. Do you think piercings are sexy?'

This one goes into various areas of male attractiveness and exactly what women consider attractive in a man.

• Do I look gay?

This one is a killer. It never seems to fail. The root could be that a guy just tried to pick you up, or your friend said you look gay in those shoes/that shirt, or you were at the bar (doesn't even have to be that night) and you got hit on by a guy. They'll laugh, and it just works like a charm.

• Do you think Derren Brown and Dynamo are sexy?

The follow-up (planting the root) is to say that you've been studying magic/psychic stuff/ESP or whatever, and that you wondered whether it was these guys' looks or their abilities that made them sexy to some women. It leads into any skill you profess to have, or any routine you can perform, in these areas.

• Do you believe in palm reading/handwriting analysis?

Follow with, 'Me too,' or 'I didn't either, but then ...' and go into a story about a relative who does it for a living and showed you some stuff. 'I was sceptical, but I brought my friend along and they got everything right. I'm not entirely sold, but I've been learning it a bit and want to see if it's a way to get to know people better, more quickly.' This is a nice way to open and lead into one of these areas in a smooth way.

Some opinion openers have more 'walk-up strength' than others. If you have three girls sitting in the corner and need to go to them to make an approach, it'd seem strange to go out of your way only to ask if they think you look gay.

That question, more spontaneous-seeming, lends itself to someone right nearby. However, using 'How soon is too soon ...?' would work very well in those circumstances. Generally, you need a more serious opener for a walk-up.

Is it lying to use these openers? I certainly don't see it that way. First, if you have something from your life that would work as a real opinion opener, then feel free to use it; it'll work well as long as it follows the format of the above. My feeling on using these openers is that it's okay to have an 'excuse' to talk to women – and I've met so many amazing women from doing just that. We don't have many real reasons to talk to women. We know what time the club closes, which bars are good and what time it is, so why not use an excuse to talk to them that's likely to lead to a good, genuine conversation?

Direct Openers

It took a while before I had the confidence to deliver a direct opener. You have to believe in what you say and put yourself on the line. You have to have complete authority. If there's even a hint of weakness and the girl picks up on it, the opener will fall flat. When you have confidence from your success with other openers, or if you're confident because you can tell the girl is attracted to you, bring out the direct opener and it'll be fantastic. You will get super-fast results and women will think you're incredible because of your boldness. With a direct opener, if she doesn't respond negatively, take the direct route and escalate quickly.

Here are some examples:

✓ I saw you and just had to come and tell you that you have the most amazing smile/energy/legs/ fashion sense.

✓ I know this is kind of random, but I had to tell you that you're just too cute.

✓ Do you know who you remind me of? Someone I want to meet.

✓ I saw you and I knew that if I didn't come and introduce myself, I'd be kicking myself all day.

✓ I like you, and I'm going to get to know you.

Situational Openers

Situational openers are what I mainly use now, after years of trial and error. When you find yourself spontaneously using situational openers, you know you have them down. This means you're well on the path to becoming a true natural.

Assignment No.3

Write down three openers you like; then go out and open ten new interactions. Your goal is just to open and stay in the conversation as long as you're comfortable, make an excuse to leave, get the woman's name and eject. This is to help you get comfortable with opening sets. You will notice that, as you become more comfortable, the interactions will last longer and longer.

A situational opener involves taking something about the current situation and using that to start the interaction. It could be noticing something about the woman you're approaching; it could be a Seinfeld-esque 'What's the deal with that guy?' Usually it's noticing something about the environment and posing the first question that comes to mind: 'How can they eat ice cream in the winter?' 'Would you wear *that*?'

In looking back on an evening, I know when I used a situational opener because when I try to remember which opener I used, I can't. It's so natural and unconscious and uncalculated that it slips my mind. The way to become comfortable being as natural as possible is to get used to saying whatever comes into your head, without delay or planning.

To see examples of hundreds more openers, go to: www. puatraining.com/openers.

6. The Mid Game

From Opener to Hook Point to Rapport

You now know how to approach. You can start a conversation with a woman and get into a conversation. Now what? What do you say? How do you prevent those dreaded awkward silences? The answer lies in a simple set of conversational skills and comfort-building techniques that can be easily mastered so that you can move your interactions from the opener to the close. I call these the 'skills of the natural'.

Any close – whether it's a number close (where all you do is get a girl's phone number), a kiss close or a sex close – requires a certain degree of good rapport and connection. With the skills of the natural, you can learn how to easily achieve rapport with a wide variety of women. For anyone who wants to become a natural with women and feel like he's always had that innate ability, this is the chapter to pay special attention to.

I used to be a terrible conversationalist. I was boring on dates, useless in groups, a terrible public speaker and unable to hold people's attention. Now I game like a natural. This means that I'm able to break down exactly what's necessary to be a naturally good conversationalist and to generate attraction. What's more, I can give you exercises to practise this skill on your own.

During the first minute of an interaction, you need to do most of the talking. Anything that puts the conversational pressure on the girl you're interested in is something that she could use as an excuse to end the interaction. When she is comfortable and committed to the interaction (which could be instantly, but generally takes longer from a cold approach), you can start putting some of the conversational burden on her.

The Art of Small Talk

Women are sick of boring conversations with men. They've had the same ones over and over and over. If you can be different, you'll stand out hugely and quickly generate attraction. But first, what *shouldn't* you do if you're a good conversationalist?

Avoid These Common Mistakes

I'm willing to bet that a lot of these mistakes will sound familiar to you. We've all made them!

• **Interviewing her**

Many women are approached and immediately put on the spot to answer a series of questions. The man's only response to her answers is usually, 'Oh really, so ...' This quickly gets boring, and any woman who puts up with this for long must either be really attracted to you or be very, very polite (or desperate).

Don't ask a series of questions. Ask one and connect on that point; then ask another. For advanced-level skills, try to elicit the answer without asking the boring question – make an assumption or guess about what she does, where she's from or what food she likes. You get the same information, but it's more interesting for her.

Hairdresser Conversation

What kind of conversation do you have with a hairdresser, a person in line at the post office or the aunt you see once every six months? It's probably boring and shallow. As in, you have the conversation but aren't really listening and don't really care, and it's entirely unmemorable. Likewise, when you meet someone totally new they typically say things like, 'What do you do?' 'Where are you from?' 'Do you like films?' Blah, blah, blah.

We all hate answering these questions over and over, yet we ask them of others! For attractive women who get approached regularly, it's even more of a turn-off.

• Stating the obvious

If a girl has pretty eyes, she's probably been told that five thousand times. Find something more specific to say to her, preferably not about her appearance. Or don't compliment her at all. It's fine to give an obvious compliment with feeling when you're already together, but in the early stages it's not what she wants.

The above methods of eliciting information may either put conversational pressure on the girl or else they're boring. Here's what you should be doing instead. The following are some ways to elicit the standard information without asking boring questions:

Ask Leading Questions

Instead of asking, 'Where are you from?' say, 'Are you Swedish?' Make some kind of personal guess that shows you're paying attention to her.

Make Assumptions and Funny Guesses

Instead of asking what she's doing, say, 'Okay, so you're waiting to meet Steve. He's a guy you met on the Internet, and you've no idea what he looks like, but he's going to be wearing a red shirt.' She'll laugh and then tell you what she's actually doing – or even better, she'll play along with it and you'll have a fun moment. Make up a silly scenario: What's she going to do with her friend? Why is she in your town?

Another example (depending on whether you're at a bar or a Starbucks) would be: 'Let me guess – so you've been shopping all day, bought loads of stuff and now your feet are killing you, so you're going for a coffee or beer together.' This kind of thing also gets you in the habit of focusing on women, making observations and cold reads. Over time, this skill develops and you can usually guess correctly!

Connect via Conversational Links

A 'link' is a transition point given to you by your conversational partner that you can use to extend the interaction without starting a new, unrelated topic. Every time a woman opens her mouth, she's giving you a link. It might be her accent, the words she uses or the information she gives you. If she tells you she's Brazilian and studying English in the States for three weeks, you have three links that you can feed off (Brazil, studying English, here for three weeks). Once you've established a connection by responding to a link in the conversational chain, you can then ask another question or elicit another link.

Your goal with each link should be to connect in a positive way, enhancing the likelihood of rapport. The best way to do this is to talk positively about her. Less effective ways are to relate the point to your own experience, to be clichéd or to be negative. Let's look at the three levels of evolution in this area:

1. Conducting a high-pressure interview

You: What do you do?

Her: I'm an artist.

You: Cool, so … where are you from?

Her: Switzerland.

You: That's nice. What do you do in your spare time?

Her: I like going to movies.

Put yourself in the girl's position here. She's constantly under pressure; the spotlight is always on her and she's being asked to contribute a lot of information while getting nothing in return. Regardless of her answer, you move straight on to the next question. This is because you're already thinking about the next question as she answers, instead of trying to use what she gives you in a unique way depending on her response. Unfortunately, this is how most guys try to connect with girls.

2. Self-obsessed relating

You: What do you do?

Her: I'm an artist.

You: Cool, my brother is an artist; he makes these sculptures out of tin foil. He made one the other day of a fish that's really cool. So … where are you from?

Her: Switzerland.

You: Oh great! I have a Swiss watch and I like Swiss chocolates. My friend went to Switzerland on holiday, said it was great. What do you do in your spare time?

Her: I like going to the movies.

You: I love watching films too. I saw that new
one with Johnny Depp; that was cool. I want
to watch that other new one coming out next
week, forgot the name ...

What's going on here is that you're using the link,
taking the pressure off the girl; so it's better than the
interview. However, you're not making a connection; in
fact, you're putting up a barrier. You're saying, in effect,
'Anything you say I will relate to my reality, and I won't
try to understand yours.' When someone is talking about
himself, it's less interesting than when he's talking about
you. In this kind of conversation, the girl won't want to
give more to the interaction because you haven't shown
empathy or understanding.

To get faster rapport and connection, you need to learn
to have conversations like this:

3. Taking things deeper

You: What do you do?

Her: I'm an artist.

You: Interesting! I like that: I imagine you
must see the world in a different way than most
people; you must be able to appreciate beauty in
more things. Where are you from?

Her: Switzerland.

You: You don't look like it, but I've heard that
people from Switzerland are quite conventional
and really stick to rules and things. You look
more like a bit of a rebel – just look at that
hairstyle! What's a hobby of yours?

Her: I like watching movies.

You: I guess that, being a creative person, you must enjoy seeing other people's creativity. But when you look at art, perhaps you always see the technical aspects as well, so it must be nice to go to a movie and just enjoy the experience.

The above dialogue uses snippets from a real conversation, but in the actual conversation I didn't jump around the topics in that way, because I was talking with and about an actual person. Because I was making an attempt both to understand her and to get things right, she opened up easily, jumping in and expanding things, and the conversation got deep very quickly.

This final example, showing how even relatively boring questions can be used effectively, reveals that learning to relate to a woman's reality is a very powerful technique.

Dance-Floor Game

Can you pick up girls on the dance floor? If you can't, you're limiting yourself severely. There are tons of girls who love dancing who you won't be able to approach. My philosophy, back and whom I was first learning, was that I wanted to be able to pick up a girl I was attracted to at any time, in any place and in any situation. As someone with two left feet, I felt uncomfortable in clubs and was very self-conscious; dance-floor game didn't come easy. Now I can dance a little bit – at least I'm on the beat – but the main thing is that I'm not self-conscious and I have fun dancing. Yes, I actually enjoy it!

There are a few ways to pick up a girl on the dance floor. It will always be more of a numbers game because it's nonverbally direct, but with a bit of practice you can up your odds.

Dance-Floor Tips

The first thing you need to do is differentiate yourself from the other guys on the dance floor. They're doing a couple of things that you should *not* do.

Do Not Do This

✓ Stand around the girls, checking them out while not dancing yourself.

✓ Make a sad attempt to dance without being into the music, just trying to get near the girls.

✓ Grind against a girl's bum.

Do This

✓ Have fun dancing around, without trying to get near the women. Enjoy yourself; enjoy the music. When you're a man having fun on the dance floor, you'll immediately stand out from all the other men. The women will move away from all the other guys (who are drooling over them, or trying to grind against them) and gather around you.

✓ You can then mirror a particular girl's dancing in an exaggeratedly funny way, get eye contact and force interest. Initiate a 'dance-off' with the girl where you gesture to her to watch your moves; then bust a silly little move and point at her expectantly.

✓   On the edge of the dance floor with girls who aren't quite dancing, you can say, 'Do you like dancing?' If they say 'yes', say, 'Do you salsa?' – and, as you say it, take them and start salsaing.

You need only about four salsa lessons to be able to do the basic steps, which are all you'll require. Trust me, you can quickly kino-escalate from the salsa opener. It works pretty much each and every time.

Structure of a Dance-Floor Seduction

The tips above illustrate a few common mistakes men make on the dance floor. In addition, sometimes men attempt to communicate too verbally, which doesn't work because of the sound level. Other times they end up simply dancing opposite their partner and don't escalate from there, so she walks off.

Here is the process for a dance-floor escalation, from seeing a girl you like to kissing her:

1. Open nonverbally (hip bump/eye contact/gesture/ other nonverbal acknowledgement).

2. Dance opposite each other for twenty seconds or so, maintaining eye contact at least 90 per cent of the time.

3. Step in closer, introduce yourself and have a very brief verbal exchange (twenty seconds max). This

will tell her that you're now in an interaction; now she won't just leave, because she knows you're interested and confident enough to talk to her.

4. Dance opposite her again and, after a short time, offer your hands; continue dancing, holding her hands in a push–pull fashion, introducing spins if you feel comfortable with them. Maintain eye contact.

Now we have some progress, but to get to the kiss close we need to slow things down. Clubs don't generally play music that has a seductive rhythm; their tempo is much too fast. That doesn't need to stop you. You're leading the dance at a certain speed, so you can gradually slow it down and get a little closer, while maintaining complete eye contact.

To escalate from this position to the kiss is easy, since 90 per cent of the work is already done. It requires only a step or two more. You can try running your fingers through her hair, or kissing her on the cheek and then moving onto the lips. Alternatively, if you can see that she's ready, just go directly for the kiss.

Attraction Building

Whether you make contact on the dance floor or use your new small-talk skills to chat up a woman at the bar, at some point she's going to want to contribute to the conversation. When she starts to ask you questions, you want to be ready. Here's how to keep things moving in the direction you want, no matter how good her questions:

Have Interesting Answers to Standard Questions

There are certain questions and conversational paths that occur again and again for each person. Think about what yours are and make your input more interesting. If a conversation gets boring because the girl starts asking boring questions, she won't realise it's her fault – she'll just know she's bored! The obvious one is, 'What do you do?' Either make your job interesting or describe it with passion; if it's undeniably dull, be brief and switch to something more interesting, like a hobby – 'But anyway, that's work; what I really like to do is ...'

Avoid These Topics

✓ Religion

✓ Contentious political issues

✓ Violence

✓ Bad past relationships

✓ Anything negative

Talk with Passion

If you can talk with passion about things you care about, your energy draws people in. If you enjoy something, let it show: be expressive, using visual and emotive language. People will get caught up in it and start to feel good too. When they feel good, they'll want to talk to you more.

A Mid-Game Case Study

Let's put it all together with an example of the natural and situational opener. The following interaction was a real demonstration for a student. I recorded it on MP3, and the transcript runs below. There are many techniques used that you can continue to refer to; you'll see more each time you look.

A girl stands alone in Leicester Square, in central London, with her arms crossed, looking pretty unfriendly.

> **Me:** Hi! You're crossing your arms and I study body language, so I could say that's because you're closed or in a bad mood; but I was noticing a lot of people standing like this recently, and either people are more closed at this time of year or more people are cold! *(Laughs.)* So are you in a bad mood or are you just cold?

> **Girl:** I'm cold.

> *I'm bantering without putting conversational pressure on her. This is necessary because I have no indication of interest and she looks unapproachable.*

> **Me:** See, people take this body language stuff too seriously. They need to put more disclaimers in these books. People crossing their arms are closed, *unless* they also might be cold. People

stroking their hair are attracted to you, *unless* their hair is in their face and they can't see anything. *(Laughs.)* You look like you're waiting for someone?

Girl: Yeah, I'm waiting for my friend.

At this point I don't immediately ask another question, like 'Who?' or 'What time were they meant to be here?' or 'What are you going to do together?' This would be natural, but not very interesting. She has given me another link that I can feed off, so I should use it. Her body language is opening up, and she's receptive to the interaction.

Me: I hate waiting for people here. You can't call them because they're on the subway, and there are so many people here you keep thinking, 'Is that them? Is that them?' The time goes way slower than when you're waiting somewhere less hectic. So let me guess, it's your old school friend and you're meeting for the ten-year reunion dinner?

Girl: *(Laughs.)* Well, it's my friend from uni, but we're going for a coffee. What's your name?

This is a big sign of interest. She's asking a question of me. It isn't related to the topic and it's personal, which means she wants to know more about me and extend the interaction.

Me: Richard, and you?

Girl: I'm Anna.

Both: Nice to meet you. *(Shake hands.)*

Me: Wow, your hands are cold. *(Takes other hand too, and squeezes them both. I've quickly done a quite intimate thing that jumpstarts a sexual frame.)*

Me: So is your friend cute?

Girl: *(Laughs.)* She is, actually.

Me: Cool. So we can all go to coffee together, but we can't stay long; we need to be somewhere. Tell her I'm your husband, that we met last week – it was a whirlwind romance – and that we flew to Vegas, got married by Elvis and came back yesterday. *(Both laugh.)*

Assignment No.4

Practise your new conversational skills on your social circle. See if you can make the women feel good and get a deeper level of connection than you normally do. You'll notice that you get a much better reaction from people and can even use these skills at work.

Push–Pull

The technique I call 'push–pull' involves mixing up an interaction. The push part is when you get closer to her and become more friendly, intimate and complimentary. The pull part is when you move away, break the connection, and seem a little disinterested or distracted.

Push–pull is great because it accomplishes a couple of things:

✓ It establishes you as high status – other guys wouldn't dare do this!

✓ It gives her an emotional roller-coaster ride, a necessary ingredient for a great pickup. (Push–pull works especially well on sassy girls – the tougher, more confident and testier the better. It can fall flat on the sweet, innocent type, so don't use it on *every* girl you meet.)

Here are some examples of lines you can use for this effect:

✓ 'You're like my bratty little sister.'

✓ 'Do you have hot friends?'

✓ 'Would you like me to buy you a drink?'

✓ 'You're too young/old for me.'

✓ 'Wow, you ask loads of questions. Do you want my CV?'

✓ 'You're a nice girl with bad-girl mannerisms.'

✓ 'You're a bad girl with nice-girl mannerisms.'

✓ 'Normally I'd be really attracted to you, but I think you're just acting cool so I'll buy you a drink.'

✓ 'Your first impression kind of sucked, but actually you're ...'

✓ 'You're the coolest girl I've talked to ... in the last fifteen minutes!'

✓ 'You're cool ... you can help me pick up chicks.'

The Hook Point and Indicators of Interest

The hook point is that moment when a girl shows interest in extending the interaction. She's clearly happy for you to stick around and talk more. You can tell you've reached the hook point when:

✓ She asks you questions.

✓ She asks your name.

✓ She gives extended answers to your questions.

✓ Her body language becomes more open.

Once you've reached the hook point, you should look for indicators of sexual interest. You'll know she's sexually interested when:

✓ She strokes her neck when in conversation with you.

✓ She looks at your mouth.

✓ She tilts her head to the side when speaking to you.

✓ Her pupils dilate.

✓ She laughs too much at your jokes, even when they aren't funny.

✓ She seems happy listening to you, even when you're talking rubbish.

✓ She holds eye contact with you and doesn't look around the room or at her friends.

   Note: if she's nervous, or if it's just not in her character to hold strong eye contact, she could still be interested.

✓ She's comfortable with your touching her and invading her space.

✓ She shows willingness to leave her friends and stay with you.

✓ She laughs and hits you on the shoulder when you tease her.

✓ She looks at you in a dreamy kind of way.

✓ She asks if you're single.

✓ She's comfortable with pauses in the conversation.

✓ She uses your name in conversation.

✓ She leans into you.

The Rapport Phase: Strengthening the Connection

In talking about the skills of the natural earlier in this chapter, I wrote about how to make connections with a woman. This continues now in the rapport phase. The difference is that the goal has become finding a reason to see her again and discovering mutual interests.

Here are some tips to help you build rapport with a woman you've connected with:

Be Observant

Notice things about her appearance (clothes, accessories, hair, nails, jewellery). Women usually put a lot of time and effort into the way they look; her bag, for example, might have been chosen to match her shoes, belt, earrings and dress. Most people don't notice such things, so she'll be happy if you do.

Furthermore, jewellery and accessories also often have a story behind them, which means they may mean something special to the girl. If you ask about that beautiful old cameo she's wearing, she may associate you with the warm feelings she has for the grandmother who gave it to her.

Talk About Things That Evoke Passion and Feeling

What is she very passionate about? It might be anything from friends and family to travel or ballet. Connect on these points by showing that you understand why she feels that way.

I've told you to avoid asking the usual boring questions. So what kind of things would it be okay to ask? The best questions build comfort and create a connection that elicits emotion. Here are some good examples:

- **Do you remember your first day at school?**

This is something that she probably won't have talked about for a long time, but it has strong emotions attached to it. To ask a question like this, you can't just say, 'Where are you from? What do you do? Do you remember your first day at school?' You need to root the question first, leading into it smoothly. You could do this by saying, 'You know, I was walking down the street this morning and I passed a bakery and smelled freshly baked apple pie. It immediately took me back to when I was six years old, and I spent the next thirty minutes walking around like a kid with a silly expression on my face because I was remembering my childhood so vividly. What about you, do you remember your first day at school?'

After she has given her response, you should connect on it. You could say, 'I can just imagine you with your My Little Pony lunch box, skipping to school.' Next, you should relate your own story.

If you can connect like this on a few emotional topics, then you've built a deep connection in a short amount of time. You'll already have talked about stuff that's not normally talked about until you've dated a girl for three months or so.

- **If you could wake up tomorrow anywhere in the world, where would it be?**

This is another good question, and it replaces boring questions such as, 'Do you like travel?' and 'Did you go on holiday this year?' This one doesn't need so much rooting; it could simply be, 'I need a holiday – let me ask you, if you could wake up anywhere in the world tomorrow, where would it be?' Connect on her answer – 'Yeah, lying on the beach, with the sun beating down, the sound of the ocean ...' – then relate your own dream holiday in vivid detail.

• Are your friends mostly men or women?

This gets her talking about people she cares about, and her response will tell you something about her character. The question is an unthreatening one with no right answer, so she'll feel comfortable responding openly.

• What's the one thing you can't say no to?

This is a good way to find out something she really enjoys. It could be chocolate – perhaps fresh orange juice. Whatever it is, it should make her eyes light up. You can then connect by describing how good it is to eat that chocolate, how it feels when you put it in your mouth and taste it as it melts. Do this and watch how you can lead her into a desiring state.

• What talents do you have that would surprise me?

This is a great question and a challenge. Early on in an interaction, she won't feel any need to answer challenging questions. By the rapport phase, though, she'll feel some pressure to respond to a question like this to prove herself to you. Remember that she's likely to ask the same back to you, so have something ready.

• Have you ever been in love?

Ask this, and then dig a bit deeper about the times she has been in love. Don't ask what happened – this would focus on the breakup! Make her want those feelings again; since she's with a cool guy, she'll probably be imagining them with you. This is a great one for a couple of reasons: first, it brings out the emotions and memories connected with love; second, it starts her imagining a relationship with you.

When you've done this, you'll already have a deep connection with the girl. On numerous occasions, many a girl has told me that after just a few hours she feels like she's known me for months. The reasons are:

- ✓ I'm completely comfortable, open and relaxed with the woman.

- ✓ I'm making her as comfortable as she normally feels after three months.

- ✓ She's feeling things that she would normally only feel within a committed relationship.

- ✓ She's talking about things she would only normally talk about with very close friends, family or a long-term boyfriend.

Build Attraction by Breaking Rapport

Breaking rapport is one of the most powerful things you can do to build attraction. When you add it to your game, you'll see a dramatic improvement.

Breaking rapport involves disagreeing with the woman you're trying to seduce on a particular point, or expressing a contrary view. To exemplify its importance, imagine being a hot woman for a moment. You are being approached by a string of smiling, nodding men, and you feel as if you can't do or say anything wrong. You could say you love cats, and they'd say they love cats; you could say you like torturing cats, and they'd say, 'Cool'. Okay, maybe that's going too far, but we all know that the natural thing to do when with a beautiful woman is to go into 'me too' mode, where you agree with her on everything and try desperately to connect. You assume that similarities will bring you closer. This might generally be true, but the 'me too' approach is what 99 per cent of men do, and you've probably realised from reading this book that it's what 99 per cent of men *don't* do that brings you success.

Imagine being that beautiful woman again. Men agree with you on everything and think everything you do is just great. You know there are things they shouldn't like about you, but they don't express those dislikes. This means you won't fully trust them: you think they're after one thing only, and so their compliments aren't worth as much.

The answer to this is to break rapport – but you mustn't do it on big things that have an emotional connection for her. Don't call her passion for painting lame, but you can break rapport on casual interests like Harry Potter books, independent films, etc. When you say that something she likes is rubbish, it makes it twice as powerful when you later say that you appreciate something about her.

If you say, 'Oh, I love Harry Potter too,' 'Oh yes, I love musicals,' and then say, 'I have a good feeling about you; we should meet again,' you come off as fake. Better to say, 'Harry Potter – I couldn't even get halfway through the first book,' 'I caught *The Lion King* but wouldn't see another musical anytime soon,' and then, 'I love your laugh.' The compliment has a much stronger effect in this latter case, because you've shown that you say what you mean and mean what you say.

You don't want to break rapport too early, though. Do it after the hook point, and just enough to show that she can do something wrong and lose you. The point is not to lower her self-esteem or make her feel stupid; it's just to show that you can disagree and that you have your own views and opinions. If you *do* break rapport, the best thing to do is quickly change the subject, to avoid turning your conversation into an argument.

Don't be afraid to tell the truth: it actually increases trust and connection as well as increasing attraction. Trust and honesty are keys to gaining people's respect. Breaking rapport is a way to be honest without hurting people's feelings. If you notice yourself 'me-tooing' and not getting as much attraction as you'd like after the hook point, try breaking rapport combined with genuine compliments – and also try challenges.

Issue Challenges

Challenges are ways to establish that you're 'the selector' (a.k.a. the high-value person in the interaction). You chose her, not the other way around. Most guys will passively let themselves be selected, so if you can challenge a woman, it'll be uniquely attractive. You need to have earned some value, however, before she'll respond and try to meet your challenges.

Some examples of challenges you can issue are:

✓ 'If everyone looked the same, how would you stand out?'

✓ 'Can you cook?'

✓ 'Are you rich?'

✓ 'Beauty is common, so what do you have to make me more and more attracted as I get to know you?'

✓ 'There are three things I look for in a woman. The first is *(insert quality – e.g. confidence)*, the second is *(passion)*, and the third is … no, I'm not telling you. *(She will almost certainly follow up with a question: 'Why not?')* … You might fake it.'

The above examples communicate that you're picky and won't date just any girl – looks are not enough. This makes you more attractive because you're telling her, in a way that comes across subconsciously, that you're high value. This is the outer-game way to challenge a girl. It's a tricky business, though: if the thoughts in your mind are about how much you want her and how you'd do anything for her, there will be conflict between your nonverbal and verbal communication.

Women are sensitive and will pick up on things subconsciously; they might not mention them or even consciously know that they've noticed, but they'll be affected positively by friendly challenging. You can start with artificial challenges such as the ones listed above, but you should aim very quickly to use natural challenges – things that grow out of the conversation.

Natural, genuine challenges do far more than simply establish you as a high-value man: they draw out a woman's character and preferences. Before I started using challenges, I got into a few relationships that were just plain wrong for me. One of the very first girls that I dated was totally unsuited to me. At first things seemed perfect because I was so happy to be in a relationship with a pretty girl (well, with *any* girl). We had romantic picnics in the park, she stayed over at my house many times and I stayed at hers. She introduced me to her friends and I did the same. On the surface, and in my mind, things were great. But after three weeks, she became difficult to get hold of on the phone and then sent me an email saying that she thought we should just be friends. She dumped me!

We were very different: she smoked cigarettes and weed and I didn't; she liked different food, enjoyed different music and had a different outlook on life. Instead of being solid in my own reality, I showed her that I would change for her. I downloaded the music *she* liked to my MP3 player and even said I'd smoke weed with her. I called her every day, and this became a problem. I was always available. She dumped me after three weeks because I liked her more than she liked me; I looked at her like I loved her, and she felt stifled.

The funny thing was that, a few months after she dumped me, I found a recording on my MP3 player; it was the last conversation we had on the last day that I saw her. My player must have accidentally switched on and been recording in my pocket. I could barely listen to it – not because it brought back sad memories, but because of how weak, needy and unattractive I sounded. I was seeking approval, validation, letting her take charge, asking her to 'please stay longer,' asking when we could meet again. It was sickening. I was breaking all the rules I'd learned and knew very well. I was doing what so many men do. Women become so important to us that this is how we act when we finally get one. The knowledge I'd learned wasn't

Get a pen and describe on paper your ideal woman. What character attributes does she have? Does she smoke? Does she keep fit? Is she a leader or follower? Is she kind and generous? Can she dance? Can she sing? Is she sharp? Is she educated? Does she read poetry or celebrity gossip? Does she like Disney films or action flicks? Does she like sushi? Is she well travelled?

Once you have your list, when you go out to meet women some interesting changes will take place:

First off, you won't be as intimidated by a girl's looks, because you'll be looking for something more – for particular traits and skills. If you can work questions that address the attributes of your ideal women into an interaction, you'll flip the dynamic. Your conversational partner will have to start qualifying herself to you. You're positioning yourself as the selector and seeing if she matches up to your requirements. Ninety-nine per cent of men don't do this, and you'll see how women start chasing you if you do.

Second, this technique will help you avoid bad relationships – the kind that are doomed to fail from the start, but that you force to work for a while because you really want a girlfriend or because this particular girl is really cute. When you understand what you *really* want, you'll know very quickly whether a woman is girlfriend material, a cool chick you can party with, or a girl you might have a sexual relationship with but nothing more.

enough to stop me from making the mistakes men have been making for centuries.

After she dumped me I was crushed for two weeks. I thought that every time I was in love with a girl, she'd dump me. But then I decided to take action: I sat down and figured out what I needed to do so that this wouldn't happen again. I never did make the same mistake; and if you complete the preceding mission, you'll avoid it completely.

Isolate for Deeper Rapport

To 'close' a girl, in most cases, you need to 'isolate' her. Have you ever noticed that conversations with large groups are very lightly topical, compared to one-on-one interactions where the subject matter can get very deep? Which conversation is more likely to bring out emotions, to help you get to know someone better and form a bond? That's why we need to isolate.

My definition of isolation isn't that you're the only people in the location, but that the two of you are the only people in the conversation. Her friends could be one metre away, or even closer – as long as they're not involved in the conversation.

For me, the easiest way to isolate a girl is to turn her away from her group. She doesn't need to leave them completely and walk away with you, just as long as she isn't looking at them.

A student once asked me to open a girl who was part of a group of six. Now, I *could* have opened the whole group, bantered for a while, won them over and then tried to isolate the chosen woman from there. But there are two reasons why I don't like doing this:

Firstly, I don't always want to exert enough energy to entertain a huge group in a noisy location. Secondly, my problem in the past has been that if I involve myself too much in the group, they all want to talk to me, and isolating one girl then becomes difficult – she feels social pressure as well, because all eyes are on her.

So in the above-mentioned case I wanted to isolate the girl 'under the radar'. Having noticed that the group had pretty much split in half, I approached, quickly established physical contact with her (turning her around by the shoulder before saying a word), introduced myself, and – lo and behold – we were isolated as soon as she turned away from her two friends.

With a pair of girls, isolation is very difficult. Generally speaking, you need a wingman in this situation. For a group of three, my simple isolation strategy is to open everyone, reach the hook point and then deliver a personal statement to the girl I like (e.g. an observation about her jewellery). The key here is to speak your isolating statement at a lower volume and break eye contact with the others. They will typically then engage each other, while the eye

Leading to Isolate

When it comes to moving from the hook point towards the close, you generally want to be leading the girl at all times. 'Let's go dance', 'Let's sit down', and 'Let's go get a drink' are all ways to lead and isolate. Others include, 'Come over into the light' and 'Let's go over there; it's less crowded/noisy/smoky.'

contact and attention you're paying the girl should ensure that she continues it with you. You next sidestep slightly around the girl and away from the other girls, so she has to turn to face you. You're now isolated. Wasn't that easy?

Take It One Step Further: Deep Rapport

Use this technique with caution. I call the closes I can get with this method 'GF-closes' (short for girlfriend). I'm careful to do this only with girls I genuinely feel something for. It's wrong to use it on those I would only consider for a casual relationship. Deep rapport is a way to get a soul-mate-level connection with the girl and go beyond anything she has ever felt before.

Achieving deep rapport is a simple two-stage process. Once mastered, it can be done on the fly with any girl. The steps are:

1. Elicit emotional content.

2. Give feedback and connect.

First I'll explain the process and then I'll give an example that illustrates how to apply this technique.

Okay, so how do you do that first step of eliciting emotional content? It's not that hard, actually. These subjects typically have emotions attached to them:

✓ Passions and interests

✓ Memories (e.g. of childhood)

✓ Future ambitions and dreams

✓ People close to us

Let's use the example of passions – the first item listed – but remember that what follows applies to all of the above. Your goal should be to get down to this deep emotional level and connect. Every person has things they're passionate about. These aren't critical 'must do' activities, but things that provide a sense of joy, achievement or simply being fully alive.

Some examples could be:

- ✓ Dancing (either watching or doing)
- ✓ Going to the theatre
- ✓ Checking out museums
- ✓ Creating art
- ✓ Playing an instrument
- ✓ Reading or writing fiction
- ✓ Going fishing
- ✓ Golfing
- ✓ Reading or writing poetry
- ✓ Collecting something

These all share common elements: they are ways that people choose to spend their time – you have passions, I have passions and the girls you meet will have passions.

Let's look at some typical ways that passions are dealt with in conversation:

Girl: Actually I practise ballet. I've done it for ten years.

Guy: Cool, you must be very flexible.

Or, in response to the girl's same comment about ballet …

Guy: Cool, I saw *Swan Lake*.

Or …

Guy: Ugh – my mum made me do it when I was a kid. I hated it.

Or …

Guy: I'd like to see you in your tutu.

Or …

Guy: Me too!

Or …

Guy: Cool, I like football.

This covers a lot of the common responses to ballet or any other passion.

Let's think about this for a second. The girl has revealed to a guy – let's say you – something that she's very passionate about. She's done it for ten years, purely out of a personal sense of commitment. And yet in all the above examples, her offer to you has been rejected. You might as well have asked if she likes oranges, because you've treated her passion in a superficial way. If you're going to take any of these approaches to things that matter, you might as well stay on superficial subjects.

Don't dismiss her passion in any of the above ways. *Connect* with her on it. You could lie and say how much you love ballet. I don't like to lie, so I wouldn't do this.

What you *can* do, even if you hate ballet, is be empathetic. Imagine why she loves to dance, what she feels when she dances. By expressing that empathy, you show that you understand why she loves ballet without saying that *you* love it. It's something she's probably never heard before from a guy, and it establishes the soul-mate connection.

My answer would be made up on the spot following the guideline of seeking to empathise with why she might love ballet:

> **Me:** Wow, that's so cool. You must be very dedicated to have kept it up for ten years. I mean, when you're young it's easy, but as you get older you get more and more commitments.

This is a standard connection for any long-term committed passion.

Or …

> **Me:** So you must really love dancing. Most people have their nine-to-five jobs and come home and watch TV. It's refreshing to find someone with a passion that's expressive and artistic.

This is standard for any artistic or creative passion.

Or …

> **Me:** People might think that dancing is just learning steps and performing them, but I think it really brings out the soul in someone. You can dance robotically by perfectly learning the steps, but it's when you really *feel* them that you become great.

I also imagine that it's a way of expressing your feelings through the movement of your body, like an artist does on canvas or a musician does through an instrument. When you're in the moment, you're expressing yourself through the way you move. It must go back to before we communicated with speech and used dance and ritual to express our emotions.

I'd love to see you perform sometime.

You can see why this is so powerful. It can be applied to any passion, whether you empathise with it or not.

Listed below are some things that you probably don't do yourself, but that doesn't mean you can't connect with people who comment about their love for these activities:

Fishing is about being with nature, experiencing serenity (being alone with your thoughts) and enjoying anticipation mixed with excitement when you catch something.

Stamp collecting is about a sense of achievement. Each stamp has a memory attached to it because it's from a different time in your life. Your stamp book is like a book of memories.

Going out and getting drunk on a Friday night is about how you've been stressed at work all week and are finally able to be yourself with your friends, completely in the moment. It's about just feeling the enjoyment without a care in the world – that sense of release from it all.

Overview of Conversational Skills

You may be feeling swamped about now, awash in techniques and approaches you need to remember. Take a deep breath. None of this is rocket science; it's just not that hard. If you can carry on a conversation, you can get a girl.

Before we move on to using touch as a tool to take you to rapport and beyond, let's see if we can't consolidate the needed conversational skills.

Step One – Mastering Eye Contact

Let's start with eye contact, that most basic form of communication. Most men either break eye contact nearly all the time, or break it at exactly the time when they should maintain it. A small number of guys have a creepy, weird or just generally bad form of eye contact that makes a woman uncomfortable. Instead of avoiding eye contact (as experience has probably taught them to do), these guys need to work on their problem.

A few things dictate how your eye contact comes across to another person:

✓ Whether you blink the usual amount of times. (You should!)

✓ Whether your head is pushed forward, ahead of the rest of your body. (It shouldn't be!)

✓ Whether your eyes are opened more than seems natural – as they might be when, say, you're surprised. If you're *trying hard* to hold eye contact, you'll end up staring, which may cause this excessive opening to happen.

✓ Whether your intent is positive and affirming. If you hate women and just want to fuck them, some of this will come through in your eyes and women won't like you. If this is you, you don't need PUA Training, you need a psychotherapist. Your intent should be as healthy and sincere as possible.

If a guy has generally good eye contact, he'll still likely break it in the following way:

Him: Hey, do you like pizza?

Her: No.

Him: *(Breaks eye contact; then allows two-second pause.)* Umm. *(Looks back.)* Right, so what food *do* you like?

This exchange might sound fine, but it's actually a conversation killer. Let's look at why.

In the early moments of a conversation, we're trying to establish various important connections, including the following types that eye contact can help with:

Hold her attention

Try the following: First, get someone to look at your foot and talk to you. Then look away and think about how it feels. Now make that person hold eye contact and talk. Look away again. When you looked away the first time, you probably didn't feel drawn back to them. The second time, you were aware that they were looking you in the eye and so you *did* feel drawn back to them.

It's important for the girl you're talking to to be looking at you, which is my definition of holding her attention. If someone you're talking to looks away, then her eyes will notice other things, her attention will wander and she won't listen as fully. (It's like when you're typing emails while talking on the phone – you can still respond, but you aren't really listening.) A girl whose attention you're not holding will soon become bored and want to leave.

Build a connection and build attraction

Our eyes are the most beautiful parts of our faces – arguably, of our entire bodies. They are attraction builders in a range of individualised colours. So picture the following two versions of the same scenario:

In the first, a couple on a first date aren't talking to each other and aren't looking at each other; they're looking around the room and at other people.

In the second version, they're still not talking, but they're looking into each other's eyes.

Do you have experience with the second version? It can be a dramatic moment, if connection and attraction are being built without words. The eyes reveal all. So when you're talking and holding good eye contact, you're achieving two things simultaneously:

1. Holding attention.

2. Building a connection and building attraction.
   (As noted above, this is also true to a similar degree when you're holding eye contact but not talking.
   So at all times you must be either talking or holding eye contact.)

If we look again at our 'Do you like pizza?' scenario, we can see that by simply replacing the break in eye contact and the 'Umm' with a pause that maintains the eye contact, the connection is maintained and the girl's attention is held. A side benefit of this is that she might elaborate or ask you a similar question in turn, a positive by-product of holding eye contact, which means you actually have to do less work in the conversation.

If you feel the need to break eye contact, you should do it when you're the one talking and she's looking at you. In a multi-person set, spread the eye contact evenly, but direct it to one person in particular if she starts to break eye contact and look away.

Step Two – Developing Self-Awareness

Next we need to focus on removing nervous tics (tapping your fingers or toes, touching your face, playing with your watch, etc.). For you to do this successfully, you'll need to either make yourself completely aware of your body when you're in a stressful situation or do one of the following: videotape yourself or have someone you trust observe you and be brutally honest in telling you what you do. I've tried all three over the years and have gone through the step-by-step process of:

1. Becoming aware of the nervous tic

2. Realising when I've just done it

3. Stopping myself *as* I'm doing it

4. Stopping doing it altogether

Step Three – Having a Comfortable Conversation

Next we have to work on the actual conversation. If you're starting from a position of silence, the first step is to say something. Most people won't make a direct statement ('That's a nice shade of red you're wearing'), but will ask a question ('What do you do?'). When I watch a guy who's had no training talk to a girl who's behaving naturally, the conversation will normally run as follows:

Guy asks question. Girl responds. Guy says, 'Cool,' or, 'Right,' or 'Okay,' and then asks another question. If there's more detail required, the question will be on the same subject: 'What do you do?' Study. 'Cool, what do you study?' Psychology. 'Oh right, what year are you in?' If there isn't much detail to gather, then he'll normally um and ah, and then switch threads: 'Do you have any pets?' No. 'Umm. Ah. Have you been on holiday recently?'

There are many problems with this structure:

- ✓ All the pressure is on her; after all, it's easier to ask a question than answer it.

- ✓ She's being asked to reveal information before she feels ready to invest in the interaction; more often, she won't want to do this and will give as little as possible.

- ✓ When she does give the guy – say it's you – some information, she doesn't feel she's receiving any reward for doing so, or that you're really listening and interested. All you say is, 'Cool,' and then ask another question.

✓ You're not connecting with her at all. You could have emailed her your questions beforehand and picked up the answers later!

✓ Generally, the conversation doesn't deviate from a predictable, prescribed sequence. You don't follow any of the new routes suggested by her answers.

✓ She's had this conversation hundreds of times before.

So what you need to do is:

✓ Take some of the pressure off.

✓ Reward her for giving you information.

✓ Make an attempt to connect with her on as many points as possible.

What you should in fact do is connect and go deeper, every time you elicit a piece of information. Remember our earlier discussion of links? You should be trying to produce a link and then using it to extend the interaction by making a statement. Every response she gives is a link. You need to be able to make a statement or observation, if possible in the second or third person, about what she has just said, and then follow it with a question.

Here's a good formula to remember:

**You speaking = 90 per cent statements,
10 per cent questions.**

Step Four – Making the Conversation Interesting
Without Running Out of Things to Say

Keeping the conversation going is a problem for most
guys. Generally we run out of stuff to say and go blank.
You might ask, 'Have you been to Miami?' She says, 'Yeah,
years ago, when I was a kid.' You say, 'Oh, I might go
there soon,' and she says, 'Oh, cool.' Then that thread has
gone dry and you need to switch subjects. There's a pause
and you've run out of stuff to say. It happened because you
connected at the lowest possible level, at the least interesting level of speech – talking about yourself in relation to a
subject she doesn't have much to say about.

Area of Conversation

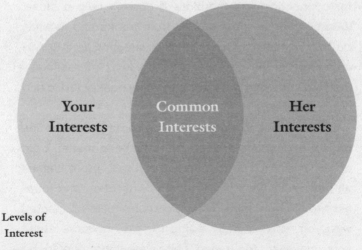

| Your Interests | Common Interests | Her Interests |

Levels of
Interest

High — Talking about her: 'I have an intuition about you …'
Talking about her in the third person: 'I usually find that artists …'
'Did you see that article in the paper the other day?'
'I went shopping yesterday …'
Low — 'My friend likes to play golf …'

If you'd directed the conversation to a more fertile area – one that connected with her – you would have got a much better response from her and thus had more to say in response.

If you do run out of things to say, you always have two options to fall back on – dropping down to a lower level (talking about yourself) or switching threads.

A Note on Storytelling

Guys often ask me how they can improve their storytelling, because other popular pickup theories place a strong emphasis on it as an important part of a seduction. Personally, I don't like storytelling as a tool for pickup, because I don't believe that a story allows for connection and therefore it doesn't help a close. Women can get great stories from books and movies, but not necessarily a sense of connection and understanding. For the most part, no story is as interesting as meeting someone you feel completely connected to and understood by.

It's worth noting here that talking about yourself is fine once a connection or attraction has been made. A girl could sit and listen to Johnny Depp talk about himself all day and enjoy it, because the attraction and interest are already there. When someone feels connected with you, she naturally wants to find out more about you; however, too much self-referencing should be avoided in the early stages, before that connection is established.

Step Five – Leading the Conversation to Solidify the Close

When you're talking to a girl, you generally want to lead the conversation. This means that you have a conscious idea of which way you want to direct it. But there are bad – unproductive – conversational areas that you want to avoid:

✓ Talking about yourself all the time

✓ Talking about dark subjects such as war or violence, which I cautioned against earlier

✓ Addressing shallow subjects – generalities like the weather, television or small talk about work

If you talk about shallow subjects, the best you can achieve is to have her think of you as comfortable, confident, interesting and possibly funny. This is great, sure – but she can find other men who have those qualities. To take it to the next level, you need to connect with her.

To stand out from other guys, I try to cover the following areas:

✓ Character traits

✓ Motivations

✓ Emotions

Anytime your conversational partner says something, think about how it might relate to these three areas. Let's imagine you just found out that she moved to your town from Europe. Instead of sticking to your usual thought process, try to filter that information through these three questions:

1. What type of person would do this? (Character traits: extroverted, adventurous.)

2. Why might she do this? (Motivations: money, following a dream, seizing an opportunity.)

3. How might she feel about this? (Emotions: apprehensive, excited.)

Kino-Escalation

The fact is, most people like to be touched. Hugs feel good. Someone touching your arm when they offer their emotional support offers more than just words.

That said, a lot of guys are afraid of touching a woman in a bar because they're scared of being perceived as creepy. Yes, women hate being grabbed by drunk guys at the bar, but if they're talking to someone they like, they *want* to be touched!

Kino-escalation is the process of going all the way from incidental touches to sex. Obviously the first time you touch a girl generally can't be when you kiss her; that'd be weird. You need to get her comfortable with your touching, and there are lots of ways to do this.

✓ *Intent.* Women can sense the intent behind kino. An arm on the shoulder from someone thinking, 'Okay, now I'm going to escalate by putting my arm on her shoulder,' will make her feel weird. She'll subconsciously know the difference between creepy touching and nice touching because she's been touched by a lot of men! When she's attracted to you, you can get away with anything you like, but until that point your intent should be pure. When you touch her, make it part of your natural movements; touch her in the same way you would touch a friend and keep the intent behind it positive and natural. Don't think sleazy thoughts! Later, when a woman is attracted to and interested in you, you can have a sexual intent behind your kino that will be completely accepted.

✓ *Speed.* The faster the kino, the more you can get away with, because it becomes harder to object to. The brain doesn't have time to register the hand on the shoulder if it's there for just a second.

✓ *Eye contact.* Do *not* look at the part of her that you're touching; that draws attention to the touch and feels 'icky' to women. On the other hand, don't go for full eye contact either. When you go to escalate kino in a major way, maybe by putting your arm around her, eye contact will make it an intensely high-pressure moment. If you're looking away when you make this move, it's much more comfortable and acceptable. Use the looking-away trick when taking a girl's hand or doing anything else that seems potentially too intimate at the time.

Kino is best seen, so watch this video guide to see kino done right: www.puatraining.com/kinovideo.

Excuses to Touch

Making use of existing excuses to touch solves the problem of kino-escalation for anyone not used to touching strangers in conversation. Below are some nonthreatening ways to kino-escalate:

✓ Don't shake her hand when introduced; hold it for about three seconds. It's long enough to notice, but not long enough to object to.

✓ Use high-fives when you find something cool about her.

✓ If she goes to the gym, exercises, looks tough or whatever, ask to feel her muscles. Flex your arm and point at her to do the same.

✓ Check out her jewellery. Hold her hand to see her rings or bracelets. Move her hair back to check out her earrings. You can use many excuses to check out her hair. 'Ever wear it up?' 'Is that your natural colour?' 'Ever had it long/short?'

✓ Take her pulse.

✓ Ask if she salsas or does any other dance and dance with her. Don't ask if she wants to; just lead.

✓ If she gives you any shit, take her hand, put it on your chest and say, 'Oh, you're breaking my heart!'

✓ Try arm-in-arm leading as you move from bar to table or dance floor.

✓ As you tease her, try friendly poking, prodding, tickling, play-fighting, nudging – all great, playful ways to kino-escalate.

Sexual Tension Techniques

Here are some techniques for heightening sexual tension that are purely physical. Others that are verbal, or a combination of verbal and physical, appear in the 'Sexual Spikes' subsection, overleaf.

✓ *Finger playing.* When you're holding hands, play with the woman's fingers and see if she reciprocates. This is surprisingly sexy and a great test.

✓ *Hand squeezing.* Squeeze her hand and see if she squeezes back. This is a great indicator that the kiss close is definitely on.

✓ *Triangular gazing.* This is a method of making her think in a sexual way. Look at her left eye, then the right, then the lips. One second on each. Repeat.

Playful Escalation vs Sexual Escalation

You can escalate kino in two ways, sexually and playfully. The best way to escalate with a friend or a girl from your social circle is to playfully test out her receptiveness, instead of making a high-pressure move to sexually escalate. Sexual escalation, as the name implies, has a sexual intent behind it. Playful escalation seems safer to girls who already know you because it's what brothers and sisters do. But it's also what boyfriends and girlfriends in a comfortable relationship do, so it's a great way to escalate and trigger enjoyable feelings of sexual tension.

Sexual Spikes

Often, you can physically escalate the kino to get a girl primed for a kiss close. But you can also use verbal escalation to get her in the mood and bring in some sexual tension. Most guys won't do it, or at least won't do it smoothly. Here are some routines and lines that can be used:

✓ 'Cool, you're my new girlfriend.'

✓ 'You look like you're imagining kissing me.' This is a good one, because it isn't asking if she wants to kiss you, but if she responds positively the kiss is on. If she wasn't imagining kissing you already, she will after this. Watch her look at your lips! Then you can say, 'Okay, now you are.'

✓ Take her pulse. Then say, 'I knew it: you are attracted to me.'

✓ When you're having a conversation, stop and look at her breasts. Check them out blatantly. When she asks, 'What are you doing?' or calls you on it, put a finger up to signal 'Wait,' then look up and say, 'Okay, carry on.' It's very funny.

✓ 'What's your favourite fruit? ... Wow, I've never eaten *(strawberries)* off a naked woman before!'

✓ 'The other day, I heard a girl get hit on by the craziest line. A guy said, "Imagine me going down on you all night." Now I don't know about you, but ...'

✓ 'How much would you like to kiss me?'

✓ 'On a scale of one to ten, how dirty is your mind?'

✓ 'If you were in kissing school, what grade would you get? Let's find out!'

The Kino-Escalation Process

All of the physical and verbal steps discussed in this chapter can sometimes be skipped and you can go straight for a kiss. That works sometimes. But to smoothly lead into a kiss, you need to ramp up the kino bit by bit.

The process below shows a smooth path from nothing to kissing. You can also combine this physical progression with some verbal sexual escalation (see 'Sexual Spikes', opposite):

✓ Touch shoulder

✓ Take hand (using excuse)

✓ Dance

✓ Hold hand

✓ Squeeze hand

✓ Touch hair (using excuse)

✓ Kiss

7. The Close

It's the moment every guy dreads – actually putting your chips on the table and going for *it*. In some situations, this will mean going for a number; in others, it will mean going for a kiss right on the spot; and, in still others, it will mean getting the girl back to your place for a night of fun. In the pages that follow I share with you strategies and tactics for all three of these situations so that when it's time to make your move, you'll know exactly what to do, and how to do it.

We begin with the first type of close: the number close.

Going for a phone number is a high-pressure moment for most guys – they don't know when to do it and they don't know whether the girl will give it to them or reject them. Even after getting a number, it can be difficult to convert it into a date or another meeting. I used to have pretty good conversations and then not ask for the number, either because I'd feel insecure about revealing that it was indeed a pickup attempt or because I'd be afraid she'd say no. But it's an essential skill to learn, and it becomes easy if you do it smoothly and repeatedly. Here's what to do.

Number Closing

Most guys make the mistake of making small talk for a period of time and then just coming out and asking for a number. This is wrong. A connection can be built quickly just on small talk, but it usually takes a lot longer. Keep in mind that the conversation needs to be directed towards the goal at all times.

Targeting Conversation for Number Closing

A conversation aimed at getting a beautiful woman's phone number needs to be based around connections and common interests:

✓ How does she spend her time? What does she do when she isn't working?

✓ What foods does she like?

✓ What places does she like to go to in the evening? Is she a party girl?

✓ Does she like the arts?

✓ Is there something she would like to do but hasn't yet tried (e.g. a salsa class)?

These are some basic common-interest questions that could lead to a possible connection. Think up your own, some in advance and some on the fly; there are hundreds of possible alternatives.

Taking two opposite examples, let me show you how to lead into a number close from a general conversation:

You: What places do you like to go in the evening?

Her: I like Club/Bar X.

You: Cool, it's good there. Have you ever been to Club Y?

Her: Not so far.

You: Well, some friends and I are going there on Friday. You should come.

Her: Yeah, okay.

You: Excellent. What's your number?

Or …

You: What do you like to do when you're not working?

Her: I like to go to the theatre/museums/ ballet/rock concerts.

You: Have you been to that new show/ exhibition/whatever?

Her: No.

You: Me neither. We should go.

Her: Okay, sure.

You: Great, give me your number.

Never ask for a number directly; it should flow naturally. The close should be assumed.

Finally, most guys get at least occasional numbers that 'flake'. This is when you get a number but when you go to call her, it's either fake or she doesn't pick up. To help minimise what I call 'flakeage', try this:

Ask her if you can enter your number in *her* phone too. Have a connection or something you can do together, as described above. And, most importantly, arrange a date there and then. If you've already arranged a date, she can be thinking about it when you call. Apply these tips, and all your good interactions should end in solid number closes.

Simple Lines for a Number Close

How about if you can't find a connection, don't have time to, or for some other reason just don't have a conversation like the above? You can use the following universal technique:

> **You:** It's been great speaking with you. We should continue this some time.
>
> **Her:** Sure.
>
> **You** *(handing her your phone):* Okay, put your number in there and we'll arrange something in a few days.

Or ...

> **You:** Listen, I need to go and meet my friends, but what's the best way to keep in touch with you?
>
> **Her:** You can take my number/add me on Facebook/email me.

Intuiting the Correct Pressure
Level for Number Closing

Knowing how strong or gentle and how fast or slow to move after you've made a connection with a new woman is all part of the natural seducer's learning curve. This applies to when you're with her in person or on the phone, to your method of closing and also to your proposition for the first date or meeting after getting the number.

If you're with a girl and ask her to meet you for an intimate romantic dinner and then come back to your house for wine, you're putting a lot of pressure on her. She'd better like you a lot! If you're suggesting that she go out to a cool party with all her friends – and you – there isn't so much pressure. Bear in mind what you're asking the girl to do. If you meet her for ten minutes and then suggest that you go on a date/for dinner/to the movies/for a drink, she'll go home, think about it and talk to her friends; and she could easily change her mind and flake. 'Will it pass the friends test?' is a good guideline to use when suggesting a meet-up. Will her friends say, 'What? You met some guy for five minutes in Starbucks and now you're meeting him alone in a bar? He'll probably spike your drink and rape you.'

You'll need a good connection so that she's sure enough of you, feels safe around you and is also attracted and intrigued by you. The easiest possible number close would be to invite the girl to a nice club or party with her friends, which may even pass the annoying friends test.

Use low-pressure closes when you aren't so sure about the solidness of the set. Use higher-pressure closes when it's really on – when you don't want to beat around the

Objection Handling

Now is a good time to mention dealing with objections women might have. This subject is almost big enough to warrant its own section, so pay attention! The situation: she's tipsy, you meet in a bar, you have a great time. Easy to see her again? Not always. The problem is, she's going to go home, talk to her friends, and be distracted by all the other guys chasing her. You can easily turn into 'the dude I met when I was drunk,' even though you might have made the most incredible connection of all time. You can be thinking she'll fall in love with you, but she'll flake!

The way you deal with this is by making statements that put the potential objection out there right away, before she thinks of it later. Consider these options:

'I know we're drunk, but I can tell that we'll get along great. It'll be excellent to meet up somewhere more quiet and really get to know each other.'

'I didn't expect to meet a great girl in a nightclub. We might go home and think that we had an amazing connection just because of the flashy environment. That might be the case, of course – but I'd love to find out by getting to know you better in a more chilled-out location.'

By preempting her objections, you help her remain focused on meeting you again and not on the potential problems. This is especially important if you escalated kino pretty hard. In that case you'll also have to deal with, 'Maybe he's a player,' and, 'If we meet again, he'll be all over me right away.' You can use the same method to deal with these issues too.

---

bush and neither does she. The personality type of the girl will be a major factor: if she's indecisive and easily led by her friends, then she's much more potentially flaky, and a low-pressure closing will work better.

Kiss Closing

The kiss closing is a sticking point for lots of guys. Going for the kiss is another point where you're putting yourself out there to get rejected. The way to remove the pressure from this moment is to work up to it smoothly with a variety of escalation techniques, and by using tests to see if the girl is ready. Think back to 'the three characters of a seduction' that we talked about in chapter 3: Mr Sociable, Mr Comfort and Mr Seducer. If you're not in the seductive character mode at the time of the kiss, she might not feel in the mood.

Here are some techniques to help make the kiss a smooth move she'll go for every time:

1. Touch her in increasingly more sensual ways leading up to the kiss:

✓ Touch her arm for emphasis when you're talking.

✓ Touch her hand. As noted earlier, looking at jewellery is a good excuse.

✓ Touch her hair. Asking if it's her natural colour/if she ever wears it up/has ever cut it short/used to have it long/or even when she washed it is a good excuse. If she's comfortable with your touching her hair and doesn't pull back at all, then she's kissable. You can go for it here.

✓ Smell her hair. Oddly enough, that's a turn-on for girls.

✓ Take her hand and hold it as you talk. If you've done some of the above, hand-holding will be acceptable at this point. Don't look at her hand or draw attention to it; just do it!

✓ Squeeze her hand and see if she squeezes back; this is another kissability indicator. No girl ever squeezes back if she isn't ready to kiss.

✓ Stop talking, pause, tilt your head and look at her. See if she's comfortable with this attention. If she is, you can kiss her.

✓ What if she turns her face when you try to kiss? Kiss her cheek and then her neck! Chances are she'll turn around and kiss you. Turning a bit isn't a rejection, but most guys assume it to be and back away. Try this alternative kissing and you can turn her on even more. It's only a rejection if she recoils – backs off and away.

So now you know how to touch her, but your moves won't be 100 per cent smooth if you're still in the same character as when talking to your hairdresser – i.e. acting like a friend instead of a lover. It's time for Mr Seducer.

2. Establish a sexual vibe as you escalate the physical contact. You do this by:

✓ Using more intense eye contact.

✓ Switching to a slower, smoother, deeper voice.

✓ Looking at her in a sexual way, looking at her lips as well as her eyes. If she reciprocates, she's imagining kissing you.

3. Sometimes, even with no work on your part, she'll want you. When a girl wants to kiss you:

✓ She squeezes your hand.

✓ She looks at your lips.

✓ She touches your chest instead of your arm.

✓ She's comfortable with hard eye contact even when no one is speaking.

Sex Closing

I believe that every girl is persuadable. I'm not going to use the term one-night stand in this discussion, because you may very well see her again, but I will say same-night sex – in other words, sleeping with the girl the night you meet her. Personally, I always try to sleep with the girl as quickly as possible, even if I'm aiming for a real relationship, because in my experience, it makes things so much easier once it's out of the way. There, I said it!

Why Same-Night Sex?

Sometimes you meet and feel a strong sexual vibe. If you took that particular girl's number and agreed to meet another time, that spark might be gone. I've had my best experiences when things seemed just perfect on the first night I met a girl. If you want a casual relationship, sleeping with her before she knows you well enough to become emotionally attached is the right policy. If you want something deeper, sleeping with her quickly so that you can both become more relaxed with each other is also the right policy.

Remember, I'm a pickup artist. I'm not grabbing a jaded, drunk chick off the dance floor at 2.00 am; I'm meeting a beautiful girl, usually the best in the club – and partway through the night I'm getting to know her, then (usually!) taking her home later. This means we can create a romantic, intimate, passionate experience. I love romance, a perfect Hollywood moment; I don't like quick sex in the bathroom. And I think you can get this on the same night you've met if you're both pretty sober and have more than just a physical connection. I've done everything from twenty minutes street-to-house with a super-hot model (the hottest girl I ever slept with) to a slow ten-hour seduction marathon with a virgin. (I wasn't being a bastard, and she eventually became my girlfriend!) The bottom line is that there are different types of same-night sex, and it generally depends on the girl.

How to Lead a Girl to Same-Night Sex

So what kind of girls tend to be interested in same-night sex? There's a surprisingly wide range, from 'ready to go'

Safe Sex

I always have condoms in my house and with me at all times when I go out. Over the years, I've come to learn two things about safe sex (and why it's important):

✓ If a girl would sleep with you with no condom, then she'd do it with other guys – and probably has.

✓ STDs (a.k.a. sexually transmitted diseases) are a serious business. Maybe you've caught something before and got better after being treated, so you think STDs are no big deal. But some STDs are incurable and can literally ruin your life. Plus, how confident can you be when you're walking around with a rash or sores on your penis? Google herpes (click on the images if you dare), and I'm sure you'll never go out without condoms again.

girls, to 'just this once' girls, to girls who protest, 'I'm not that kind of girl.' Each kind of girl requires a different response from you.

'Ready to go' girls

There are some girls who have same-night sex often, and with lots of different guys – in effect, one-night stands. These girls are not only open to same-night sex, they want it. What appeals to this type of woman is a dominant man who looks like he can take care of her sexual needs and desires. If you want to be that guy, you should make outward displays of confidence, approach directly and escalate smoothly from touching to kissing, telling her what you want to do with her, etc. With this girl, you can simply lead her out of the club and there won't be many, if any, questions asked about what's going on. 'Grab your jacket,' you can announce, 'and let's get out of here!'

'Just this once' girls

Other girls may have gone along with same-night sex a few times before, but it isn't something they're automatically agreeable to or normally into. They're not sluts and they don't want to be treated as such. Still, they enjoy sex and aren't prudish.

These girls need more than the physical, however, and will reject you if that's all that's on offer. You can give them a taste of sexuality, but you should also slow down to show that you have self-control and take the time to get to know each other.

This type of woman needs to feel that Hollywood moment; she needs to feel like she has really met a fantastic guy. Stare into her eyes in a loving way; find out stuff about her and connect on it. Then show her that you're becoming more and more attracted to her as you find out more and more about her. Even as you're connecting with her on an emotional level, however, you can be conveying sexual tension in the way you look at her. In summary, turn her on intellectually, emotionally and physically.

Often, you'll need a reason for this girl to come home with you – hearing you play a song, seeing some photographs you took on a recent trip to someplace she wants to visit or your cute little dog. Try telling her simply, 'Let's go somewhere else,' and then, if and when she asks where, you can say, 'I want to show you something.' Head for your place, though, even while you're talking. If she objects to where you're taking her, you can say, 'Well, you can't stay long, because I need to wake up early,' and then quickly change the subject. *Do not engage in logical debate*. Keep leading her and then change the subject.

You need to read her objections; if she objects to you verbally but still consents physically (for example, she says she shouldn't go back with you but is still walking hand in hand), it's usually a token objection and can be quickly dealt with. However, if she objects to you physically and verbally, *immediately stop* what you're doing! She is not going to go home with you or do anything with you – and you need to respect her and stop it there! *Learn this important point*. Women sometimes like to playfully object and wrestle with you if they want to be controlled. This can make it difficult and confusing for men, because sometimes women really *mean* their resistance. You need to make sure you are always respecting the woman and that you can read the difference between token objections or hesitations and definite resistance.

'I'm not that kind of girl' girls

The third type of girl is the one that's not very sexual and will always react in horror at the thought of a 'dirty' one-night stand or of sleeping with a guy so quickly. These girls can often be persuaded to have sex, but you need to carefully read the signals she gives you.

Connect with her on an emotional level first. Introduce a tiny bit of sexual tension, but just enough to generate attraction and to avoid being thought of as merely a friend.

Getting her back to the house won't be too difficult, because you'll generate trust and you *won't kiss her* before you get there. After you've connected with her on all levels, suggest going somewhere more quiet, more comfortable, where the drinks are cheaper, to chat some more – whatever. You need to talk about future plans with this girl, things you can do together. If there are any objections, you should manage to get around them with, 'I want to show you where I live. Anyway ...'

Once you get to the house, sit her down on the sofa or on your bed. Get the wine out. Give her time to get comfortable. After five minutes, go in for the kiss. You could have kissed earlier because you had comfort, trust, connection and attraction, but you waited to avoid the 'Oh, I'm horny now; let's go to my place' vibe. The kiss has been 'on' for a while, so it will be easy.

Escalate very slowly and smoothly from that first kiss. Anytime you sense discomfort on her part, take a step back – show her something on your laptop or put a movie on – keep it there for a time and then reescalate. When the time feels right, offer an excuse to get in the bed (it's more comfortable); have an excuse to take clothes off (it's hot) – all the while physically escalating. It's got to be like it happened by accident. Once she's naked, the interaction has most likely passed the point of no return and should be smooth sailing. Remember, you must learn to read the woman. If she objects verbally and physically you need to stop what you are doing and only re-escalate if she is clearly encouraging.

Girls in this category will be much more likely to go home with you if you don't directly mention the fact that they're going back to have sex with you. Of course, they'll know it on some level, but a much higher percentage of girls will sleep with you if you make the subtle shift from 'Want to go

Dirty dancing is generally good for getting in the mood, getting her comfortable with you physically, etc. You need to be confident and comfortable so that she feels that vibe too. Treat her like your girlfriend. Touch her with familiarity. Awkwardness won't fly.

back and have sex with me?' to 'Want to come for coffee?' Other lines that work well include 'Want to go someplace more comfortable?' and 'Let's go somewhere else.'

The difference is that you're leading, not asking. People feel more comfortable in simply following rather than making a commitment to follow. For example, 'Let's go dance' always works better than 'Would you like to dance?'

Sex on a First Date

For a lot of reasons, you might opt for a number close or a kiss close over same-night sex. That doesn't mean you're out of luck, but you've got to know what you're doing to move forward.

Most guys who meet girls for dates after a number close see the attraction completely fizzle out; or, at a minimum, they have to work through a number of dates to get into a position where they can take things physical. That's an avoidable problem. If you arrange to meet a girl for lunch or in a coffee shop in the daytime, your first date clearly isn't going to end up in bed.

Solid Closes and Buyer's Remorse

When you're getting on well with a girl in a club or a bar and there's the potential for things to get physical, there are different ways to play it. You may have heard of something called 'buyer's remorse', which in the context of dating is where you escalate the physical stuff too quickly with a girl and then she regrets it and doesn't want to see you again.

Let me illustrate this with an example. I approached a hot girl in a club one night and in a short span of time we were kissing and touching very sexually, almost to the point of getting thrown out. Wanting to slow things down a bit, I stopped, took her hand and led her to sit down. On the way, though, a friend asked me to take a picture of his group and I got engaged in conversation with him; she, probably anxious about how quickly things had been advancing, went back to her friends and ended up leaving the club without talking to me again.

If I had managed things differently – if I had sat down with her and spent twenty minutes talking and discovering things I liked about her before getting all hot and heavy, she probably wouldn't have run away and I probably would have succeeded in getting her to agree to a follow-up date.

So basically, you have to do a couple of things if you're getting physical with a girl you'd like to see again. If there's no chance of your sleeping with her that night (because she has to drive friends home, or whatever)

and you really like her, don't spend the whole night kissing her; back off and talk, then kiss a bit more, then talk
a bit. Mix it up. If you can sleep with her that night, go for
it and spend some quality time afterward.

So how do you do it? There are a few essential elements
to the sexually successful first date:

First, arrange to meet at night. There's more of a sexual
vibe at night, so you can establish a physical connection
straightaway. And meet somewhere near where you live,
preferably within walking distance. I arrange this with
a girl by saying something like, 'Let's meet at the local
Starbucks. When's good for you – 8.00 pm or 9.00?' The
question offers illusory choice on a point that's irrelevant
to me in terms of the result.

When you meet her for that first real date, the most
important thing to do is immediately treat her as if she's
your girlfriend. Kiss her on the cheek, take her hand or
put your arm around her and lead her off to the location
of your date. Remember that if she actually shows up for a
date, she's attracted to you; that's a given. By treating her
as your girlfriend, you're basically triggering all the feelings within her associated with guys she's dated for years.
You're touching her like her ex-boyfriends did. If you're
comfortable, she'll be comfortable. If you're uncomfortable and nervous, she'll be the same.

When you arrive at your destination, let her sit first and
then sit next to her. You'll be in danger of losing a sexual

vibe if you sit opposite her. In terms of conversation, mix playfulness, teasing, the sexual vibe and comfort-building. For my first dates, I always like to take the girl to a spot that closes at 11.00 pm, so it's natural to leave then and just lead her to my house.

If you don't have a favourite place that closes down early like that, you can say, 'Let's go somewhere else,' and simply lead her to your home. When you're walking down the street together, don't talk about where you're going. If she asks directly, you can say, 'We're going somewhere more comfortable,' or 'I know a great place where the music is better,' or even, 'I'm going to show you where I live.' You can also have a quirky excuse to take her home, like 'Come and see my cat do back flips.' (But if you go that route, you'd better have a cat waiting for you when you get home!)

One of the key things here is to try to distract her. Draw her attention from your destination by asking or talking about something else. 'So, did you see that new movie with Matt Damon?' Then continue leading her and walking. If she objects to you verbally but is still walking with you, don't engage in logical debate. Remember that a woman has both a logical and an emotional mind. Her emotional mind is expressed through her body and her logical mind through her speech. Distract her logical mind.

When you get back to the house, sit her down (on your bed if possible) and give her some space. Don't get in her face right away. You're doing some crucial things here – primarily, showing that you have self-control. This generates trust, and she'll feel more comfortable with you.

After a few minutes, go into the seductive character again and build some tension before you kiss her; that will make the kiss more passionate and will turn her on. Kiss for a bit, then lay her down. If she isn't in your bedroom, give her the grand tour. Have something in your bedroom that you can look at together – a photo album, say – and do that sitting on the bed. Remember, though – if she gives a strong objection, like saying, 'Stop!' or pushing you away, you'd better stop whatever you're doing (or trying to do) immediately. If she gives you a more subtle objection, or you sense one coming, go back one or two moves and try to turn her on some more. If you make sure you're respecting your date at all times and are carefully reading her signals, it should work out fine.

Sexual Confidence

A lot of guys have some performance anxiety when it comes to sexual confidence. I certainly did when I was starting out, due to knowing that any girl I met likely had *way* more sexual experience than I did, and also from a lack of confidence about how I looked. I was scared to get naked and wasn't confident in my skills!

Despite my lack of confidence, it took only a few weeks of practice to get into some great situations with beautiful girls. I'd got so good at the early stages that girls often thought I was a 'player' and probably thought I was an amazing lover because of my confidence in the first minutes of an interaction. Little did they know that I had kissed fewer than five girls, even though I was twenty-five years old!

I remember one particularly attractive French girl I met at a local bar. I got her number and actually managed to get her on a date a few days later. My 'sex on the first date system' – still in the draft stage back then – was running like clockwork. We were sitting in my room on the bed (the only place to sit in my small portion of the shared flat), and there was a beautiful moment when she revealed something very personal. She told me that she played the harp and that she thought of her harp as a 'he'; when the window was open, 'he' would make sounds from the wind that she thought was him talking to her, and she would come play a response. She told me that she'd never talked with anyone about it before, but that she felt I understood her – in fact, she said, it was as if she'd known me for months.

I put my glass of wine down, moved towards her, ran my fingers through her hair, and went in to kiss her. When she turned her head to the side, instead of backing off I kissed her cheek and then her neck and then gently turned her head back towards me. To my surprise, she went crazy and jumped on top of me, kissing me aggressively and biting my lips. This had never happened before – not even close! I couldn't handle it and didn't even like it. She looked like she wanted to devour me, and I was just plain scared!

I'd had only slow, soft and tender moments in my brief romantic career, and this girl wanted the opposite. She wanted a confident, dominant man. I'd probably seemed to be that guy when I picked her up, but I didn't yet have the sexual confidence to back up my posturing. I got on top of her and pinned her down, but my movements were tentative because I didn't really know what I was doing. She wanted me to control her physically and loved it when I managed to do that. I'd never ripped a girl's clothes off and had wild sex before, but I was game to try. I was way too slow for her liking, though; and although we did get it on, I was in my head all the time, thinking about what I should do to make her happy and not really enjoying the moment. I caught a confused look on her face at one moment, as if she was wondering what the hell I was doing.

I felt like a real man would have been able to handle the situation properly. I'd sensed that I wasn't very 'manly' for a while. When I was at work during those early years, from about eighteen to twenty years old, I was the 'friend' who posed no sexual threat, who didn't project any sexuality at all. I'd sit around with the marketing department girls and they'd talk about sex and personal issues as if *I* were a girl. When I was with my guy friends, I didn't talk about sex or women in the usual crass way. I still don't think it's necessary to do that – but it *is* necessary to be sexually confident and to be able to handle sexually aggressive women without being scared off. Women should see you as sexual, not as a gay best friend!

I'd been brought up by my mother with no male influences or role models, and I guess I lacked a general manliness and (especially) sexual confidence. I had taught myself the attributes of an alpha male and definitely projected them in a club, but I had a weak underbelly that revealed itself in the bedroom! The French girl I was just talking about was only nineteen, but I couldn't handle her. She said, in both words and action, 'I like sex,' and was very matter-of-fact about it. I was happy to have slept with her – she was one of the best-looking girls I'd met in London – but I didn't know how to give her what she wanted! She didn't come back for more, and this was going to be a big problem if it continued.

In the months that followed I struggled with how to get this area of my life handled. I'd never openly talked about sex with friends; I'd always felt uncomfortable when the subject came up. Seeing the need for change, I decided to make a conscious effort to talk about sex with male and female friends alike. Gradually I got comfortable talking about it, making sexual innuendos and jokes and being more open. I deliberately spent some time with the most sexual girls around and started regularly going to strip clubs. Within a few weeks I had a girlfriend who was a dancer. She was super confident – a half-Greek and half-Brazilian woman who was paid by the club to teach the other girls 'pole tricks'. She was totally confident with her body, walking around my flat naked, even when there was a chance that my flatmates might see her. She told me what to do in bed, what she liked; and after dating me for a few weeks she told me I was good.

Finally I'd graduated! In the days, weeks and months that followed, I brought my newfound confidence into my relationships, and now it carried all the way through to the bedroom. The most important thing that I realised was that potentially embarrassing issues could be overcome if I confronted them directly. It's a lesson that was important for me to learn and one that I hope you keep in mind as you go on your own journey.

8. The Day Game

You've now got a system for approaching and seducing a woman at nighttime – a system that will serve you well. However, you are not *always* in a bar or club when the woman of your dreams passes you by. In order to have total choice of women and the maximum amount of opportunity, it's important for you to understand how to meet women during the daytime, and how to maximise those encounters.

Day game and night game are different, and you'll probably prefer one or the other. There are benefits and drawbacks to each. Day game takes you outside of bars and clubs and into streets, shops, the gym, public transportation, etc. Day game allows you to approach girls who are on their own (as they probably won't be at night!) and who aren't used to getting hit on – at least, not in these daytime situations. That means they won't be armed with what I rather callously, but honestly, call 'bitch shields'.

In other words: you'll be getting the real person.

Most people, both men and women, have a persona that they adopt in a club or a bar. Because with day game you're both sober, on your own and being yourselves, any contact number you get in the daytime is usually pretty solid. Girls often flake on club number closes because either they were drunk when they gave the number or they don't like the idea of meeting a guy in a bar. Daytime approaches are the opposite: they're actually romantic, and a woman feels better telling her friends that she's meeting 'the guy who chatted me up in the post office' than telling them about 'the guy I met in a bar on Friday night'. There are also lots of attractive girls who avoid going out at night because they don't like nasty men groping them, don't like loud music or just prefer to do other things. If you want to meet a nice girlfriend who won't cheat on you and isn't a party girl who likes getting drunk, day game is the way to go.

A Complete System for Day Game

The problem with day game is that the girls you approach will be more difficult to hook. Girls in the daytime are doing something; they're on their way somewhere, waiting for someone, buying something or doing their workout. In the evening you can open any group standing around in a bar, and holding them for a minute or two shouldn't be too much of a problem. On the other hand, a girl walking in the street at midday will stop for you only if you've got a very good reason (asking if you should dye your hair – that old bar standby – generally won't cut it!) and it will take a lot for you to distract her from whatever she's doing.

Day game is a more advanced skill because it works best when you can use something spontaneous and situational to start the conversation. Canned material, opinion openers, routines and magic tricks seem a little weird in the day. In other words, day game is really more about your natural conversational skills and personality. One of its biggest drawbacks is that it's difficult to kino-escalate. A one-minute kiss close in the daytime is an advanced-level skill.

When you start day game, expect it to be tougher to get a good response immediately after your opener. Remember, these women are on their lunch break; they're catching a train; they're shopping. It's not like in a bar, where at most they're having a conversation with friends. It's not a sociable environment; they're not hoping or expecting to get picked up.

So don't expect to be greeted with a happy, smiling face when you open your mouth. You might very well have to work for a few minutes to warm things up and get a woman to commit to the interaction. It doesn't mean that she's rude. You'd probably do the same thing if you were in her shoes. On a girl standing still, it's fine to use an opinion opener – it's easier to hook, and harder for her to completely ignore you. But if you're stopping a moving woman, it's tough because she's already engaged in something other than you.

In fact, stopping a woman already engaged in motion is the hardest day-game skill of all to pull off. If you find yourself in this situation – if you see a woman whose looks call out to you as she strides along – you need to communicate your intent when she's about three or four metres away. You can do this in various ways:

✓ Make eye contact with her.

✓ Make a curious face, as if you're going to ask her something.

✓ Lift the palm of your hand towards her, slightly above waist height, to subtly show her a 'stop' sign.

If you wait until she's within one metre to do any of these things, she won't stop because her guard will be up. You need to deliver your opener when she's further away, to give her time to stop before she passes you.

Further tips:

✓ You definitely need a pre-opener. Use 'Hey' or something similar, and not 'Excuse me,' because you don't want her to think you want something from her (as a street beggar would).

✓ Don't go too quickly into your opener. If possible, get her to *stop walking* as you say, 'Hey … I need to ask you a quick question.' If you move quickly into your opener, it's more likely she'll keep walking as she listens and then just throw you a quick answer over her shoulder.

Your goal during day game is to fill the first minute with statement-based elaboration on the opener or a similar subject and then make the interaction increasingly more personal.

Staying on the opening subject for too long after this will make the interaction go stale, and it will get harder and harder to keep things interesting and to make a transition.

Day-Game Progression

Impersonal Opener

Conversation starts impersonally and then becomes increasingly more personal.

1 min
2 min
3 min
4 min

You

5 min

Her

In order to close, you need to make a connection between you.

As soon as you've got her committed to the interaction, get off the opening subject.

Once she's invested in the interaction, it's time to take it personal. This can be done by introducing yourself, asking what she's up to and using other questions to elicit information about her. This part of the conversation should still be structured correctly (as described in the discussion of night game), so that there's an attempt to connect rather than simply asking question after question.

The next task is to go for the number close. The way you do this is to connect with her about an activity. Some examples:

You: Do you like dancing?

Her: Yes.

You: Have you tried salsa?

Her: No. I want to, though.

You: Oh, well – I go to this great salsa class on Wednesdays. You should come!

Her: Yeah, sounds good.

You: Okay, give me your number and I'll text you the details.

Or ...

You: What do you like doing when you aren't working?

Her: Mmm ... visiting art galleries and stuff like that.

You: Cool. Have you been to the new Michelangelo exhibition at the museum?

Her: Not yet, but I've been meaning to go.

You: Well, I was going to check it out sometime soon too; let's go together.

Her: All right. Great.

You: I could do Tuesday or Friday afternoon – is either one any good for you?

Her: I'm free on Friday.

You: Cool, let's do it. What's the best way to get in touch with you?

Her: I'll give you my number.

Or ...

You: Do you go out to clubs?

Her: Yeah, sometimes.

You: I get invited to some really good parties. You should come out with us sometime – bring your friends too.

Her: Yeah, okay.

You: Cool. Well, give me your number and I'll be in touch closer to the weekend.

Or …

You: What are you up to?

Her: Shopping.

You: Do you know your stuff when it comes to fashion?

Her: Definitely!

You: Well, I was hanging out with a fashion consultant recently and she gave me some great ideas. Next time you're out shopping, I could join you for an hour and you could help me get some new clothes.

Her: All right.

You: Cool, let me take your number and we can arrange it.

Sometimes it might not happen so smoothly – in other words, the close might not arise from the conversation naturally. In that case, you could use a hook from earlier to close later. For example, you could find out that she likes shopping, art galleries and sushi in the first two minutes; and then, five minutes later, you could use any of these things to lead smoothly into the close. The intervening time is spent developing a stronger connection or just increasing her comfort (and thus the likelihood of getting her number).

Example: Complete Day-Game Pickup

The following is an example of a day-game pickup from open to close, with a range of various possible answers covered. Remember that this is a guideline; ideally, there will be room for banter or for the conversation to go in a different direction. This is principally an example of structure and shows that, regardless of what a girl says in response to your opener, you can still continue the pickup and close.

Day-Game Number Closing

A lot of guys ask me things like, 'How long should I stay in an interaction?' and 'How do you get a number close in the daytime?' The first question should answer itself: you stay until you feel you have enough mutual connection/attraction that she'll want to see you again. Generally, a solid close will need ten minutes in the daytime, but you could be as fast as three minutes. The idea is that you open and, as soon as she commits to the interaction, you switch into connecting mode and moving towards the number close.

It's important to note that the point at which you can get a number close is not the same as the point where you can

Hey, do you know where Trafalgar Square is?

(Question asked of two young women in London)

Yes, it's there.	No.
Are you sure? Because I've been sent this way and that way *(point)* and have been walking around for half an hour. I can usually tell if someone is lying, so look at me and let me ask you again, where is Trafalgar Square?	Oh really, are you tourists? **Yes.** Hmm, you look Swedish, am I right? **Yes/No.**
It's that way.	*(Use country hook to connect if possible.)*
Okay, cool, I can tell you're telling the truth. Since you know where you're going, I should definitely hire you two as my tour guides. And you can help me with something else. I'm meeting my friend in a little while. Is there somewhere around here where they do nice Italian home-style cooking? It all seems to be tourist restaurants.	What's the best thing you've done so far in London? **Blah blah.** Oh, I've done that/not done that. It's funny how when you live somewhere you never do all the tourist stuff.
Blah blah. *(At this point, you hopefully have hooked the set and they are comfortable talking to you. The next stage is to take things personal and lead towards a close.)*	How long are you here for? **Blah blah.**
What are you guys up to?	
Blah blah blah.	
My name's Richard, by the way. And you are ...?	

Do you guys like to go to clubs?

Okay, cool. Well, I'm meeting my friend later and I think we're going to a party someplace. I'm not sure where it is, but it sounded cool when he told me. You should definitely come.

(At this point, assess receptivity. Are they up for coming or not? If they are ...)

Cool, well give me your number and I'll text you the details after I meet him.

get a date with the girl. She might willingly give you her number, but then – as with some women you meet at night – flake on the date. There are different levels you can get to:

✓ *Hook point.* She's comfortable talking to you and commits to doing so for at least a short time.

✓ *Email close point.* She doesn't feel comfortable giving her number but is happy for you to have her email address. She might also take your number when you suggest taking hers.

✓ *Number close point.* She responds positively to the number close suggestion.

✓ *Date close point.* This is where she's enthusiastic about meeting you for a date, to the point of chasing after and trying to close *you,* or is showing a lot of 'IOIs' (a.k.a. indications of her interest).

The question is, what can you do, if you get only as far as a number close, to make sure you can line up a date? Some guys convert only 10 per cent of their numbers into dates; others are closer to 100 per cent – and that's of course where *you* want to be.

When you're going for a close, there's a checklist of things that will show you how likely it is that you'll get into a date:

✓ You arrange a date/next meeting there and then, for a specific activity on a specific day at a specific time and place.

✓ She takes your number after you take hers, or calls herself from your phone.

✓ There are some IOIs and attraction on her side.

✓ She asks if you always do this (picking up women
   in the street), if you're single or some other
   verbal IOI.

✓ You know that, when she's challenged by her
   friends to tell them about you later, she knows
   enough good things about you to paint you in a
   positive light.

✓ She's sure enough about you to contradict her
   friends if they say it's a bad idea to meet you.
   This means putting in the time to make a solid
   connection.

If you can check off all these items, you're in a very solid
position and the likelihood that she will flake is low. To
minimise that likelihood even further, try to make sure
that your follow-up game is as solid as possible. It will help
your success rate to spend some time with the next chapter, which focuses on the matter of follow-up.

There are different levels of number closing in day game
as in night, and this may result in a massive variable in your
success rate. Asking a girl to meet you for dinner creates
much more pressure than inviting her out to a party with
her friends; therefore, you'll need to put in a lot less work
if you're just trying to get her to a party.

There's a filter that applies like this: when she's sitting
at home with her friends and you text her, how happy
is she going to be to receive that text, and what will her
friends say about the upcoming date? If you've spent just
five minutes with her, the chance that she'll meet you one-
on-one is slimmer than that of her going to a party with

you and her friends. If you instant-dated her at your first meeting and spent an hour with her already, then the one-on-one meeting is a lot more likely. There's no benefit to rushing the close, and the contact number you get doesn't mean much if it isn't solid.

Additional Resource

If you want to see for yourself how day game is done, then you're going to want to check out our new advanced day-game video programme. It contains over ten hours of live 'infield footage' where we show you actual approaches and then break them down for you step-by-step. For more information on the programme go to the following URL: www.puatraining.com/daygame.

Day Game: Your Best Bet for a Nice Girl

With a one-on-one student, I was training one day in Trafalgar Square, in central London. I was getting the student to do some approaches when a very cute girl walked past, about five metres away; I waved and she waved back. For a minute or so I debated whether to go after her or not. When she slowed down to type a text message, I took that as my sign and ran after her. I told her exactly what I was thinking – that I hadn't been going to run after her, but then she slowed right down and I just had to. I chatted about the nearby National Gallery, why she wasn't at work in the daytime and other small talk. Then I said I'd left my friend alone and should get back to him, but that we must meet up. Her name was Melissa. I took her number and tentatively set something up for two days later. The student was impressed, and I was very happy to get such a fast number close.

I called Melissa later and we arranged to get together in the evening. We met at an underground station and I took her to a local bar. Despite my growing experience, I hadn't known that it was possible to have a date like this or to meet someone like her. She listened to what I had to say and asked penetrating questions that showed she was listening intently, really wanted to know more and was very intelligent. That kind of tuned-in listening is something I do too when I'm really interested in someone, and it was an amazing situation. Within a couple of hours, we got to know each other at a deep level that really should have taken months. It turned out to be the best date I've ever had, and the most intense connection I've ever had with a girl. Since that day I've always emphasised that there are some girls who never go to clubs and who you can meet only in the daytime. If you never do day game, you'll never have a chance to meet these gems.

9. The Follow-Up Game

How to Keep Women Interested After a Number Close

Getting a number close is a great accomplishment. As we've seen, though, it's no guarantee of an actual date – and certainly no guarantee that you'll see action later. Things aren't entirely out of your hands, however; how you conduct yourself in the follow-up will in large part determine a girl's response.

Let's look at some of the options you have for communicating during follow-up – and the advantages and dangers of each.

Text Game

Questions about texting a girl come up time and time again when I'm training guys. I used to be the worst possible texter, with most of my numbers flaking. Now my text game is very solid; it doesn't ever let me down.

Text game is actually pretty simple, and if you follow my rules for texting you should notice a big difference right away. If you don't want that prized number to turn into a flake, pay attention:

- ✓ Use only one question mark per message.

- ✓ Your messages, unless scripted, should be shorter than hers.

- ✓ Use a 'fire-and-forget' strategy – send the message, put the phone down and do something else.

- ✓ If she texts you back, take your time before responding. Don't rush right over to the phone. Take at least as long to reply as she did.

- ✓ When you write a message, leave it as a draft for ten minutes; then go back and read it again – and make sure it's not embarrassing!

- ✓ If she asks a question (like 'How's it going?') to which you can give only a boring response – don't answer it.

- ✓ If she asks multiple questions, don't answer them all.

- ✓ The best time to send a text message is when you're busy or on your way somewhere. It shouldn't look like you spent too long thinking about what to say. It should look like you finally got around to it and are answering nonchalantly.

✓ Don't use xoxo's or smiley faces ... ever! Even if she does.

✓ Never send two texts in a row within forty-eight hours without a response.

✓ If she doesn't reply, wait at least five days before trying again.

✓ Don't try to arrange the date on the first text; this is usually instant death!

Finally, for examples of actual text messages that you can send, go to: www.puatraining.com/textgame.

Phone Game

Some guys prefer getting on the phone. My friend and longtime wingman, Anthony P., is one of those. But it's a lot tougher to talk to someone when you aren't face-to-face, so when you get her number, it needs to be as solid as possible.

If you call after a number close and she answers enthusiastically – it's *on*. With a couple of minutes' chat, you can probably set up a date pretty easily. If you call and she's a bit cold or noncommittal – 'Who? Oh yeah ... I remember ... umm ... hi' – try to be as interesting as possible. Tell a story, talk about cool things that are happening and then end the call before she does. In this circumstance, do *not* try to arrange a date. Leave it a few days and call again. Keep doing this until you call and she seems genuinely receptive. She'll wonder why you haven't asked her out, so just keep building her interest; then you know she'll say yes when you finally ask.

Here's how you should structure your phone game. Once you've finished up the greeting and you sense that she's receptive, try a few of the following:

✓ Reestablish your initial connection – use call-back humour, making her laugh again at the same things as during your interaction or show her that you remember things she told you. (*'How was the trip to the zoo with your nephew?'*)

✓ Get her into a positive state and ensure that she feels comfortable. A first phone call after a nighttime number close will *not* feel immediately comfortable; it will take some effort on your part.

✓ Get a sense of her plans for the next week.

✓ Suggest something you can do together.

✓ Arrange the logistics and settle the date.

✓ Talk for a little longer and then end the call first.

If you call and get voicemail, it's usually better to hang up and send a text. If you do leave a message, make it quick so you end the call before the recording time runs out. If you plan on calling her back in three days, don't tell her, 'I'll call you in three days.' Just say or text her something short and sweet like, 'Okay, talk to you soon.' Leave her wondering if and when.

The best time to call is when you're on your way to a date, when you're on a high after a successful day at work or when you've just had some good gaming results. You will naturally sub-communicate attractive qualities that are very tough to fake (you're busy, you're high-energy, you have choices, you're not needy or outcome-dependent).

Don't plan the call for three hours and make it from your bedroom in total silence. It's better to be walking down the street or on your way somewhere. If you sense that she's about to wind up the call, head her off at the pass and say that you'd better go. It's all about maintaining control.

Facebook Game

Lot's of guys like to try to game online, but not me. I don't think it's the way to improve your game skills, because it keeps you within your comfort zone and it takes up a surprising amount of time. It's also virtually anonymous, so people never really know who it is they're dealing with.

I do use Facebook, though, and when you number close a girl via FB there are different levels of connection:

✓ It's so solid that you know you'll see her again.

✓ You *think* you'll see her again, but there is potential for her to flake.

✓ You're not in a position to get a very solid close.

If you close the girl and then add her as a friend on Facebook, something interesting will happen and you will need to be prepared.

First, you need a good profile picture. My page has photographs of me from all over the world, with hot girls, with a bunch of martial arts black belts (they were my cousin's belts), with a cute dog, flying a plane, etc. Trust me, your new 'friends' are definitely going to look through all this from time to time, especially when you add new photographs. So do this fairly often, because it will help to create more intrigue and interest. It's something that I've learned to do, with much success.

Over a couple of weeks, my new girl sees when I add new photos, new friends, etc. Now, even though we haven't had our first date yet, we're almost a social circle! She sees my face every day when she logs in on her *friends* list. She knows what I'm up to. It's better and more efficient than a daily text. After a few days, she's primed for some direct Facebook messages or maybe even an invitation to a 'safe' event like a night out with a bunch of other people from Facebook. Often she'll even initiate that contact. While I've received notably varying responses from girls that I have closed and added to Facebook, the technique is definitely fun and worth adding to your repertoire.

10. Commonly Asked Questions

We've been through all the steps of an effective pickup and you're just about ready to go out on your own – as a natural at attracting women. Before you do, let me try to anticipate some lingering questions you might have.

What's the right way to use a wingman?

I talked a bit earlier about having a wingman. 'Winging' is what I call it when you're working together with a friend to meet girls. That collaboration can greatly increase your chances. If you're alone you can approach lone girls, and you can approach groups to try to isolate a particular girl. But it can sometimes be tricky, especially when you're first starting out. On the other hand, if you're with a wing, when you approach a pair of girls you can isolate almost immediately and don't have to hold a large group for a long time. Together you should achieve more. Sometimes one of you will have to talk to girls you're not attracted to so as to allow the other one his opportunity, but it all balances out.

There are various ways to wing together. Some of the best approaches are these:

> *'Spontaneous' involvement.* Both of you stand near the girls, having fun together and reacting to what each other says. Then open the girls, seemingly spontaneously. In the following example, the first sentence is said (loudly enough to be overheard by the girls), while the second includes the group: 'No way! Hey girls, do I look gay? He just said I look gay in this shirt!'

> *Tag-teaming.* One of you approaches and opens the whole group; the other wanders in once the group is hooked. If it's a pair of girls, you can both isolate. With a bigger group, one guy should take on the group while the other one isolates the girl he's interested in. This could be either the guy who opened or the one who comes in later. With a mixed group, I find it's best for the first of you to open the guys first and make friends with them; while this is going on, the wing comes in and takes the girl.

> *Accomplishment intros.* 'This is my friend; he has the coolest job – he lives and works at the bottom of the sea, repairing oil platforms!' What you're doing is making your friend sound cool in some way. If he

did that himself, it would be bragging, but if you do it it's fine.

Where's Michelle? A pickup artist I know called 'Toe Cutter' came up with this one. It's a way of making sure you have your wingman when you need him and *don't* have him when he would just get in the way. The wing comes into a group you're already part of and asks if you've seen Michelle. You say you think she's over there and point in some direction. He turns to leave; if you want him in the interaction, you pull him back in and introduce him. If not, you let him go.

Code words. You can work out code words with your wing: for example, for location changing ('I like this song'), taking the girls home ('Want some chewing gum?') and identifying your girl ('This one is trouble').

While clubbing with a wingman can be great fun, it's important to have fun with your wing(s) in a nonclub environment too. Do competitive fun activities together – sports, games, arcading, bowling. Harness upbeat, high energy. If your only connection is skulking around looking for chicks, your relationship won't be as interesting – or as useful with women. Find some stories to tell, have loads of fun and then bring the party to the location.

What if she says she has a boyfriend?

In your mission to attract, you're going to get plenty of objections from girls. How you deal with these is very important. Many objections are just tests to see if you're enough of a man. Women are looking more for your attitude here than what you say. After looking at the examples that follow, you can develop the right mental frame to come up with your own objection responses.

Sample Responses

> **Girl:** I have a boyfriend.
>
> **You:** Cool, he can make us breakfast in bed.

Or …

> **You:** You've got a bore-friend?

Or …

> **You:** Good, it'll give you something to do when I'm busy.

Or …

> **You:** Excellent, he can hang out with my girlfriend when *we're* together.

Or …

> **You:** Nice. Anyway … *(Continue seduction.)*

I should add the disclaimer here that you shouldn't mess up people's relationships lightly. You'd be treading on dangerous ground. I personally haven't messed up a good relationship, and there are no girls out there who hate me for breaking their heart. My morals mean I get laid less than I might otherwise, but I can genuinely say I love women and don't want to hurt them unnecessarily.

Types of Girls with Boyfriends

The first type of girl who raises the boyfriend objection acts like she's single, even if she says yes when you ask if she has a boyfriend. If despite her verbal response she's grinding against you, expressing interest and showing no compunction whatsoever about flirting, she's obviously not in a relationship that she seriously cares about.

The second type shows signs of interest but seems kind of torn. She often acts nervous and unpredictable; that's because she wants you but doesn't really want to cheat. This girl is not in an *amazing* relationship, but she likes the guy and has morals. She can easily be persuaded to develop the interaction with you if you slowly build comfort and stay far away from the subject. If you take things further with this girl, you need to consider whether you're doing the right thing, because, unlike girl number one, she probably wouldn't cheat with just any guy.

The third type is the rarest of them all. In fact, it took me a few hundred approaches before I encountered this kind of girl. She has fun with you and laughs a lot, and together you have a great interaction. *But* there's absolutely no sexual tension or indication of interest. She's not looking at you in that way at all; you might as well be gay or a girl. The reason she can hold herself apart like this is that she's in a very solid relationship. She knows that no man can show her more in thirty minutes than her boyfriend has in the months or years that they've been together. Even if you're better looking, funnier and everything she's looking for, she's just not thinking along those lines at all. This is a very nice girl; you want one like this for yourself when you develop a proper relationship. They're rare, as I mentioned; you won't find many in clubs.

How do I get into an exclusive club?

Okay, so you can get into the semi-exclusive clubs and you can get into the places where you know someone. But how do you get into the bigger scenes, like the celebrity after-parties? The first thing to know about these things is that there are some normal people in these places; the guests aren't *only* models, millionaires and celebrities. The owners and managers at the club will have some guest-list power, and often so will important promoters. But let's assume you down't know any of these people.

So how do you get in? Here are my four secret methods revealed:

1. The girl with the clipboard is at the door. You approach and give her the name of Ben Harris 'plus one' – and you're the 'one'. She checks her list, and while she's doing that you take a surreptitious look at that list. She finally says you're not on it, of course. You step aside and make a quick call on your cell phone, then go back and tell her it's actually John Doe – a name that you just saw on the list. This one works in limited cases.

2. You're near the entrance, but not in line, and the clipboard girl is facing the line, meaning she's at a ninety-degree angle to the street. If you go to the door, you'll be asked what you want or told to go to the back of the line or to move away. But if you go towards the door while pretending to be on your mobile phone, you might be able to get far enough past her to see over her shoulder. So get on the phone and go up to where she is and take a quick look at her guest list. Spy some names; then get in the line and use one of them.

3. Many nightclubs use marker pens to mark people who go outside to smoke. You can buy an ultraviolet pen or whatever they use at that particular club on eBay. Hang around the entrance (using the mobile-phone trick) when people go out to smoke, and see if you can figure out what mark or letter the club is putting on hands. Go away and put the mark on your hand; then hang around outside for a bit before going in. This works best at peak times, when club employees are swamped. If the club is using a stamp, try getting someone to press their hand against yours to transfer it.

4. This method is the nastiest. You get in the line and start moving forward. When you're about three minutes from going inside, ask a friendly person in line to keep your place. Walk towards the back while seeming to write a text message. Pick a guy and look at him, surprised. 'Hey Matt, how you doing?' 'I'm not Matt,' he says. 'Really? What's your name; I'm sure I've met you!' 'Will.' 'Hmm – Will, maybe.

What's your surname?' 'Fraser.' 'You know what? The connection will come back to me. I definitely know you from someplace. I never forget a face. I'll see you inside.' Finish your text and then get back in the line; and when she asks your name, you're Will Fraser. Don't feel too bad about Will: he'll get in too, even if he's questioned, because he'll have the proper ID!

How do you walk up to a girl in a club and kiss her instantly?

I started trying this about a year into my gaming, but it took a long time for it to happen successfully. It took me many more months to figure out what I was doing so that I could teach it to other people.

This is one skill that definitely belongs in the advanced-skills section, because it's difficult and has certain prerequisites. You can't run before you can walk, and you can't instant-kiss close until you can:

> Force an IOI and go in directly following a positive response.

> Create sexual tension and escalate smoothly to the kiss in less than fifteen minutes.

Once you can do the above, the process for the instant-kiss close (a.k.a. k-close) is relatively straightforward. Here's what you do:

> Identify the girl you're attracted to.

Make eye contact; look at her like you want her and walk directly towards her, slowly and smoothly.

As you get right up close to her, take her hand, run your fingers through her hair and slowly and confidently move in for the kiss.

The reason this works is because you're creating sexual tension from a distance, using seductive eye contact. When you then walk directly towards her, she's forced to either accept (hold eye contact) or reject (break eye contact). You must be walking *directly*, however; otherwise the fact that she holds eye contact doesn't tell you anything. You must do it slowly to create the sexual vibe – the rhythm of sexual tension is slower and smoother than normal movement. So good luck!

To see this technique in action, go to: www.puatraining .com/instantkiss.

Do you use online dating?

I haven't put much energy into online dating. I've met only one girl via the Internet and would rather focus on live situations. This, however, is just me. I love the game of seduction, and, for me, the online version seems a bit watered down. When you gain command of the skills described in this book, my suspicion is that you will feel the same way.

Having said that, I *do* get a lot of questions about online dating, so I've taken the time to build a killer profile that works like crazy. It uses the principles of the natural art of seduction to draw women in, and I've had students use it to land very hot chicks. Here's the profile of your desired woman:

> She knows what she wants and isn't afraid to go for it; she likes her man to be a man but still be able to show his emotions. Balance is important to her; she works hard enough but her job doesn't consume all her energy. She enjoys the nice things in life, but is also spiritual and doesn't get fully caught up in the quest for material goods. She wants a man in her life, but doesn't *need* one. She knows that she and her man will be worth more together than apart. She enjoys the simple things in life but can also be spontaneous. She likes to travel to far-off places, relax on sandy beaches under a hot sun and then cool off in the sea, but she also likes the hustle and bustle of a busy city. This contrast and balance are part of her character. She is centred and content, but being with people that she cares about is important to her. She is kind and considerate and would like to be her naturally caring self with people who have earned her trust. She wants a man who understands her – one she doesn't need to tell what she wants, but who just *knows*. A man who can be the closest person to her, to help her make decisions and to always be there and offer her his strength when she needs it. She doesn't expect to find him right away, but she'll know when she does.

You'll see that it says nothing about *you;* there's no point, because everyone will be saying the same thing, so it's impossible to stand out. By talking about *her*, you make the profile more engaging. (As I said earlier, women are more interested in hearing about themselves than listening to your story.) Furthermore, you're qualifying her, and challenging her all the way through. If she reaches the end of the paragraph and thinks she measures up, she'll want to claim her 'prize', which can only mean contacting you.

My other dating profile was a lot shorter but still got lots of responses: 'Be careful: I'm trouble!'

Conclusion

My journey over the past five years has been turbulent, full of emotional ups and downs, but I'm incredibly thankful for it. Each month saw new challenges, situations that scared me and changes taking place within me. I wasn't always sure that I was on the right path. I didn't know whether I should change so many aspects of myself. At times I thought I might be becoming strange, and at other times I worried about becoming overly cocky and arrogant. In the end, I managed to find balance and peace – and for the rest of my life I'll be able to look back at what I was like before and be happy for making the choice to take action.

In the preceding pages I've laid out a roadmap for you, so that you can achieve your goals a lot quicker than I could. Some of the things that I did by accident *you* can do *consciously*. Mistakes I made and outline here *you* never need make.

Before leaving you to start the process of becoming the best man you can be, I want to give you two very powerful final pieces of advice – advice that will all but assure your success.

People often ask me, 'What's the one thing that helped you the most?' It's a tough question, but I can identify two things that ensured the success of my journey.

Observing Naturals to Learn Their Skills

The first is that as soon as I decided to improve this area of my life, I forced myself to seek out and learn from people who were better with women than I was. Rather than socialising with people just like me – nervous guys who were inept socially and inexperienced with women – I found the top tenth of a per cent, and I spent as much time observing them as possible.

I never had a guide, someone to tell me what to do at every step. I did, however, have these role models in the form of the people I sought out and became friends with. People like Steve and Alex. Steve is a natural with women and the greatest seducer I've ever seen. Over and over again, I've watched him pick his favourite girl, approach her without rejection, and within minutes be kissing her – and then leave the club with her. He has no idea how he does what he does – he's a true natural – but I learned a great deal from watching him.

Soon after meeting Steve, I took a trip across Europe, visiting thirteen countries over two months, and I came back a different man. I suddenly had the perspective of a man who had slept with countless women, rather than the limiting beliefs that I'd had just months before. The things that Steve did in nightclubs, the way he seduced women, I started doing almost unconsciously. Now I teach my students how to do the same exact things and how to get the same results that Steve got.

One night I saw a guy in a club. He stood out for me because he was surrounded by hot women. I'd been gaming for a year by this point, and usually in this situation would have tried to steal his girls or make him look bad in some way. That night I so admired his work that I actually decided to talk to him. Alex Kay is his name, and we became best friends.

Alex is a social superstar who can make anyone like him within minutes of meeting him. He has a huge social network and is the opposite of me: he's a natural extrovert, incredibly funny and loves the spotlight. After we'd been friends for a few months, I went on a date with a girl; and at one point in the evening she said she'd been laughing so much that her stomach hurt. I realised that by spending so much time with Alex, I'd become funny. I'd changed from the boring guy girls didn't want to see again to a guy who always had incredible first dates and great conversations with women he'd just met.

The lesson: *Surround yourself with people who have skills that you lack; learn from them and absorb their talents.*

Seizing Opportunities as They Present Themselves

The other thing that helped me the most has been my ability to take action. Over the past five years I have been presented with innumerable situations that ranged from scary to downright terrifying. Things like:

✓ Speaking in front of seven hundred people

✓ Going on live prime-time television to be interviewed by a sharp, smart-arse host

✓ Approaching women in the street in front of sceptical journalists

✓ Going to a super-high-end nightclub for the very first time

✓ Approaching groups of five to fifteen women while whole bootcamps of students watched

✓ Moving to a new city where I didn't know anyone

✓ Approaching the most beautiful woman I've ever seen – at a bus stop!

A funny thing happened when I started taking action. It used to take me hours or even months to pluck up the courage to do something; now I actually seek out scary things and commit to them right away. I recognise that feeling in my stomach that held me back for so many years. Now I have so much evidence of feeling that feeling, taking action, and thereby improving my life that now I actually *enjoy* feeling it. It means I'm going to learn something – probably something that will greatly enhance my life. The good news now is that not very much scares me; I'm comfortable in pretty much any situation.

The lesson: *Take action whenever it presents itself, whether agreeing to go out to a party, even if you're tired, to signing up for a class, to doing something drastic like moving to another city or country.*

A Letter from Richard

Dear Reader,

Congratulations! You've made it to the end of this book, and that's something you should be proud of. Now the real work begins.

I've showed you the path. It's up to you to take your first steps forward.

Ralph Waldo Emerson famously said, 'Do the thing; have the power.' In my opinion, truer words have never been spoken. And while I hope you've enjoyed reading this book, my greater hope for you is that you will *take action* on what you've learned to bring you the life you want with the women you want.

From personal experience, I can assure you that just studying won't give you what you want. Sure, it's a great way to start, but if you want to achieve radical success with women ... if you want to get this area of your life completely handled ... it's going to be the *action* steps from this day forward that determine your future.

In chapter 2, 'The Attraction', we got to the root of what causes women to feel attraction and discussed the steps you need to take to ensure that you're sending the right signals to them – signals that do in fact trigger attraction. We also laid out a series of action steps, including belief change exercises, state conditioning, body language recalibration and more. I urge you: do the exercises I've laid out for you. I have included them in this book for a reason – they worked for me and changed my life. I want the same for you.

In chapter 3, 'The Seduction', we really turned up the heat and dived headfirst into the art of becoming a natural with women. In that chapter and those that followed, I delivered more techniques and tactics than was probably sane or reasonable – but I did it because I want you to be armed with the best of the best material when you get out there. Which brings me to my next point …

Actually get out there! I know it can be scary. I know the negative voices can creep into your head and try to discourage you. But please don't listen to them. Pick a few days a week and commit to going out. At first, just commit to something as simple as physically walking into a social gathering where women are present. Then, once you feel comfortable with that, make the next step and do your first approach. As time goes on, put one foot in front of the other and remember to never give up. I can assure you, your situation is nowhere near as bad as mine was, and yet today I have everything I've ever wanted in my life when it comes to women. And I have it all because I refused to give up. I encourage you to follow in my footsteps.

Okay, that about does it for now. On the next page we have some information on the training programmes we run all across the world, if you'd like to train with us live.

Until then, thank you so much for taking the time to read this book!

I wish you extraordinary success with women from this day forward, and I look forward to meeting you in person soon.

Cheers,
Richard La Ruina

Resources

At PUA Training, we offer a number of coaching programmes for men who want to become naturals at interacting effectively with women:

The Weekend Bootcamp

The world-famous PUA Training Bootcamp will transform your life forever. In this high-intensity programme, you will spend the entire weekend with my team of Master Pickup Coaches as we go over the entire system from start to finish and then hit the 'field' for live pickup sessions during both day and night. Watch as master instructors show you how it's done before your very eyes; then put your new skills to work under the watchful eye of a coach. Nothing in the world compares to live in-field training with the pros! For details and the upcoming schedule go to: www.pua training.com/livetraining.

The Seven-Day Platinum Residential Intensive

This programme is the definition of intensity! Come live with our team for seven days and go through our intense in-field immersion experience. You will eat, sleep and breathe pickup, and by the end of the programme you'll be a natural – a pickup powerhouse. You will be training with us one-on-one for the duration of the programme, and the entire curriculum is customised for *you*. Want total transformation? This is the programme for you. Admittance to this programme is by application only. For more details go to: www.puatraining.com/platinum.

Master Pickup Artist Phone Coaching

Work one-on-one with a coach who will help guide and mentor you through whatever challenges in the game you may be facing. Have some questions about what you've read in this book or watched on the Internet? Having trouble getting past specific 'sticking points' and need specific advice? Want someone to help you set goals and hold yourself accountable? Phone coaching may be the right option for you. For more details, go to: www.puatraining.com/phonecoaching.